Al Needham Band at Halloween

DiRTY STOP OUTS GUIDE TO 1960s Chesterfield

By Pete Dodd

Pete Dodd asserts the moral right to be identified as the author of this work.
A catalogue record for this book is available from the British Library.

Published by ACM Retro
www.acmretro.com
.

Other titles in this series:

Dirty Stop Out's Guide to 1970s Manchester.

Dirty Stop Out's Guide to 1970s Liverpool.

Dirty Stop Out's Guide to 1970s Coventry.

Dirty Stop Out's Guide to 1970s Barnsley.

Dirty Stop Out's Guide to 1950s Sheffield.

Dirty Stop Out's Guide to 1960s Sheffield.

Dirty Stop Out's Guide to 1970s Sheffield.

Dirty Stop Out's Guide to 1980s Sheffield.

Dirty Stop Out's Guide to 1990s Sheffield.

Dirty Stop Out's Guide to 1970s Chesterfield.

Dirty Stop Out's Guide to 1980s Chesterfield.

Dirty Stop Out's Guide to 1980s Coventry.

Dirty Stop Out's Guide to 1980s Chesterfield Quizbook.

We're on the look out for writers to cover other UK towns and cities
and we're always on the look out for great retro photos!
Please email us at **info@dirtystopouts.com** if you fancy getting involved.

www.dirtystopouts.com

Dronfield's own Dave Berry
(second from left) on stage
in the early 1960s

Dirty Stop Outs Guide to 1960s Chesterfield

By Pete Dodd

Chesterfield was pivotal to the future career of Joe Cocker (front) who was still performing as Vance Arnold in the early 1960s.

Chubby Checker performing 'The Twist' – the song that caused a sensation in Chesterfield in the early 1960s.

CONTENTS

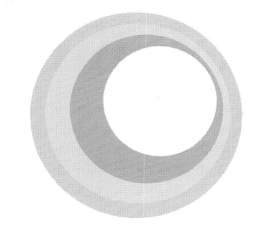

Famed local trumpet player Al Needham and fellow musicians kept the masses entertained at the Victoria Ballroom for much of the 1960s.

As a pointer to what was to come, Buddy Holly visited Chesterfield on his way to play two shows at Sheffield City Hall on March 4, 1958. He was checking out the town market before going on to Sheffield to check in at the Grand Hotel, but resisted dropping into Wakefield's Army Stores (to his left) for a snake belt, a pair of monkey boots or some sailors' trousers.

O f all the post WW2 decades, the 1960s stands out like no other. It was a time when the dull greys of post war life were driven out by the inrushing tide of psychedelic pop colour, a time of profound cultural change as society – particularly the younger end – shook off the drab dreariness of 1950s austerity.

Rationing had stopped only a few years earlier and the last conscript started National Service in the autumn of 1960. It was the decade to be young – just ask anyone in Chesterfield that lived through it. Sexual freedom and youth revolution went hand-in-hand with a massive consumer boom and increasing affluence as the post-war economy finally struggled to its feet.

Never before, or since, has a generation swept away all that came before on a wave of eager exuberance. Resistance was inevitable but futile.

As girls' hemlines got shorter with the advent of the mini skirt, and boys' hair got longer in defiance of convention, the older generation looked on despairingly and forecast the total collapse of morality and discipline.

But there's no doubt the 'Swinging Sixties' were a much-needed tonic for the nation who had lived through turbulent times during the first half of the century. And it was music that was at the emotional and spiritual heart of this irreversible movement. Rock 'n' roll, imported from the USA in the late fifties/early sixties, provided a unique opportunity for home-grown talent to embrace it and turn it into something new.

With the Beatles at the vanguard, suddenly the world was transformed into a global village. Everything was up for grabs and thanks to some adventurous local spirits (take a bow in particular,

David McPhie) much of this amazing music reached Chesterfield. There's no doubt Chesterfield was punching well above its weight – Jimi Hendrix, Pink Floyd, Small Faces, the Kinks, The Equals (featuring a peroxide blond Eddie Grant), Jethro Tull, Traffic and Free all strutted their pioneering stuff in town.

Live music fans growing up in the shadow of the Crooked Spire enjoyed an unprecedented series of shows from artists that became among the biggest acts in the country and the world.

By the latter part of the era the town was becoming a big draw for the young people of Sheffield and the surrounding area. The likes of King Mojo and the Esquire – hugely popular Steel City teenage clubs that had boasted tens of thousands as members – closed their doors for the last time and Chesterfield's home-grown venues became the 'must visit' clubs.

The first worldwide dance craze of the era (and don't forget it was only a few years earlier that all young people found it necessary to have ballroom dance lessons before joining the dating game!) was 'the Twist'. The 1960 Chubby Checker hit caused a sensation in Chesterfield as it did everywhere else.

Many critics were horrified by the 'provocative' style of the dance, which went on to many more moves including the Jerk, the Pony, the Watusi, the Mashed Potato, the Monkey, the Funky Chicken and the Hully Gully (of which more later).

The 1964 launch of pirate station Radio Caroline caused a music revolution as it circumnavigated the then stranglehold record companies had on the airwaves. Style icon of the era Sandie Shaw, proved shoes didn't have to be a female obsession as she adopted a barefoot stance when the UK was actually able to win the Eurovision Song Contest.

Meanwhile, in January 1963 the President of France, Charles de Gaulle, announced the French veto on Britain's application to join the European Common Market, the forerunner of the European Union. De Gaulle said the British government lacked 'commitment' to European integration. What goes around comes around, Monsieur Le President!

An obsession of a different kind centred around motorcar ownership; it was the true symbol of affluence – and continues to be. Car ownership more than doubled in the era and 1960 saw traffic wardens let loose on the streets of the capital for the first time. They didn't mess about. Over 300 tickets were issued on their first day on the job! The traffic regulations came thick and fast. MOTs followed a year later and the 'breathalyser' was introduced in 1967.

So don your rose-tinted spectacles and join us on a retro journey in the *Dirty Stop Out's Guide to 1960s Chesterfield*.

Chesterfield Market Hall – home of the original Hudsons (far right)

CHAPTER 1

BIG MAC AND A MUSHROOM

Geraldine and David above the shop.

T here was no-one more significant in bringing the full impact of the swinging sixties to Chesterfield town than David McPhie. Born in 1941, he was already a fully fledged young dude-about-town by the time the sixties dawned. He had absorbed the big band sounds of the thirties, forties and fifties and experienced first hand the late fifties surge of American rock 'n' roll. David, known by many as Mac at the time, was ready and waiting for whatever came next. And what a lot that was!

It's difficult to imagine that this mild-mannered, softly spoken gent would be at the local vanguard of one of the biggest cultural upheavals of the last 100 years. His quiet disposition masked a huge enthusiasm for music, which drove him to adopt so many different roles.

He drummed with the Blueberries (Chesterfield's first beat group recording artistes with their version of Ike and Tina Turner's *It's Gonna Work Out Fine* b/w Don Covay's Please *Don't Let Me Know* on Mercury Records in 1965), he managed bands and acts – including having a significant hand in the legendary Joe Cocker's early career – he was a popular DJ around north Derbyshire and South Yorkshire, and he went on to promote major acts, notably at the Victoria Ballroom's Velvet Underground club. He also acted as booking agent on behalf of others.

And his record shop, Some Kinda Mushroom, became the place to be for all self-styled aficionados of the burgeoning music scene.

David McPhie: "In the early sixties my own band, Chesterfield's Blueberries, was in its infancy as a rhythm 'n' blues outfit, and ours and Joe Cocker's paths were to cross regularly over the next five years or so, playing fairly frequently at the same venues around Sheffield, Derbyshire and South York shire; pubs, clubs, The Esquire, The Mojo, Sheffield University, etc.

"I was also involved in other aspects of the music business in the area, being resident DJ at Chesterfield's Top Rank Victoria Ballroom, opening the Smokestack Club at Queen's Park Hotel in Chesterfield (with John Fleet of Dave

Berry's Cruisers), The Velvet Underground club at the recently closed Chesterfield Top Rank (booking bands of the calibre of Jethro Tull, Family, King Crimson, Free, Fairport Convention, etc), working at Hudsons Record Shop, and subsequently opening my own Some Kinda Mushroom in Chesterfield (and briefly in Sheffield), and managing other bands, including the locally popular Shape of the Rain."

Some Kinda Mushroom
The seminal record shop Some Kinda Mushroom, named after a lyric in Jefferson Airplane's *White Rabbit* song, immediately became an oasis with a magnetic draw for young music fans and players desperate to hear and learn about the exciting emerging sounds of the time. Many of them would get to operate on both sides of the shop counter.

So notorious was the shop that the nearby girls' grammar school St Helena's declared it 'out-

St Helena's girls' school – just round the corner from the 'den of iniquity' that was SKM.

St Helena girls outside SKM challenging the out-of-bounds order placed on the shop by the headmistress Miss Clarke.

of-bounds' but a group of St Helena schoolgirls posed outside the shop in defiance of the 'exclusion zone' imposed by their headmistress!

David McPhie:
"During our years on Newbold Road we were lucky to have some knowledgeable and valuable assistance. Mick Twelves features elsewhere as a musician and bass guitarist for numerous bands, and followed me from Hudsons to SKM. He was very open and customer friendly, but there wsere certain things that 'came with the territory', time keeping being one of them (he's known as 'Ten Past Twelves' to this day).

I can remember a couple of occasions when we were on holiday, and I phoned up for some information, around 11am or 12pm, and there was no reply – late riser and designated key holder MT still being in bed. There were other issues too. These related to what I will politely term 'romantic interludes' in my absence, and during opening hours (use your imagination)! But, all things considered, you still emerge well 'in credit' Mr. T.

"John Savage and Ian Millar, another two very knowledgeable helpers, also shared my enthusiasm for (in particular) the American music of the sixties. Between the four of us we were able to provide a fairly comprehensive fund of musical knowledge for our customers. As a result, in addition to selling records, we were a 'talking shop' and debating society, with the occasional heated argument thrown in for good measure.

"Weekend regular Ian Millar was also a valued member of the 'Shape of the Rain' team as co-roadie with either Bob Oscroft or Dave Brookfield. Rob Haslam (one half of the Velvet Underground

Light Show team) was also a regular Saturday helper, and another knowledgeable contributor to our team as was Richard Taylor (But more of him later)."

"Later addition Stuart Smith (now proprietor of the Zebra menswear shop) was still at school when he joined us for some part time work, and brought with him some knowledge of the soul and disco music that was becoming increasingly influential in the UK. Stuart was later to inherit the Some Kinda Mushroom name after I had first of all passed the business on to Rob Cupitt (the other half of the Velvet Underground light show) after moving it to Stephenson Place.

"I was very into Tyrannosaurus Rex, The Incredible String Band, John and Yoko and used to buy IT, Oz, Frendz and everything else I could afford with my pocket money."

"The decision to move to Stephenson Place, a more central position, but considerably more expensive in rent and rates, was not a good move for the 'alternative vibe' of the original profile of the business. But my decision to opt out a few months later there was due to a genuine desire to move on to pastures new, and the book business soon became an attractive alternative option.

For keen young student of music Richard Knight (then 'Ricky') SKM was the place to be:

"My idea of being 'In with the In Crowd', when I was 14 in 1969, was listening to David McPhie and Mick Twelves discussing Jefferson Airplane's *After Bathing at Baxter's* or the Velvet Underground's third album behind the counter at Some Kinda Mushroom.

"I'd spend forever leafing through the album sleeves. I was very into Tyrannosaurus Rex, The Incredible String Band, John and Yoko and used to buy IT, Oz, Frendz and everything else I could afford with my pocket money. Dave's shop and presence was a very important cultural reference point for me at the time."

Richard also remembers his excitement when he noticed that the shop was about to open: "It must have been the beginning of 1968 I first saw 'Mushroom' appear at the bottom of Newbold Road.

"I was in the car with my dad, driving up past the shop when I saw it. I insisted he stop the car. Eventually, he did stop somewhere near Scarsdale Hospital and I ran all the way back down. I stared at the windows (there was barely anything in them – I think a copy of IT) and the Arts Nouveau script of the shop name. I got it. I knew what was coming. I could hardly wait for it to open.

"First chance I got I bought a copy of IT and became a regular fixture in the shop, thumbing through box after box of album covers, studying each one, learning cover art and line-ups, track lists and lyrics, labels and genres. I think I spent every Saturday in there for the next four years, and quite a lot of weekdays."

John Ashforth was another teenager keen to absorb as much about music as possible: "Some Kinda Mushroom was complete escapism. The matt black interior must have created the right ambience for imaginations to wander. Even in school uniform you felt part of the scene. You didn't need to ask for records to be played, as you wanted to hear what David was going to play next. We owe so much to David McPhie."

Richard Knight with Wini Turner a friend and St Helena's student.

Shambles Record Shop

John Ashforth also remembers a record shop in the Shambles in the late sixties, specialising in underground music. He recalls it sprang up from nowhere and disappeared back underground soon afterwards.

John: "We would hang out there sometimes after school before getting the bus home. I don't remember the shop's name (Could it have been Star Trak? – Ed.) but I'll never forget the entrancing girl who worked there. For me she was the IT girl of Chesterfield, the town's own sixties icon. She introduced me to Love. Sadly, not the passionate type or even the platonic kind, but her favourite band from Los Angeles led by Arthur Lee.

"Whenever I hear *Forever Changes* I'm usually back in that record shop, in school uniform.

"What was such a being doing here in Chesterfield? Jane, I was the tall dark haired schoolboy in grammar school uniform (the blue of Foljambe House) with nice eyes and pimples. I forgave you long ago for not fulfilling my mid-teen romantic fantasies. I'm sure it wouldn't have worked out between us anyway because I preferred the Band."

Geraldine and David got married around the time he was gearing up for the Some Kinda Mushroom project. His decision to get spliced in white (way

before John Lennon, of course) he now confesses was a publicity stunt. It worked:

"Someone alerted the 'dailies' to this publicity ploy, for that is what I am ashamed to say it was, with the (possibly) less than noble purpose of promoting our music agency and my mobile DJ career. As a result it made the pages of at least a couple of the 'red tops'!

"Our car at the time was a Hillman Minx, which was painted in bright purple for the wedding, with red and yellow flames adorning the wheel arches.

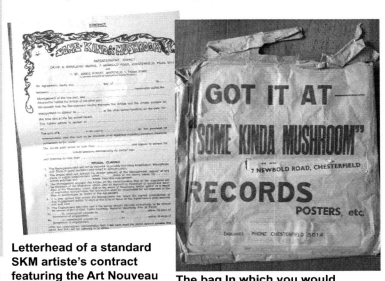

Letterhead of a standard SKM artiste's contract featuring the Art Nouveau script that was also used for the shop's sign.

The bag In which you would transport home your newly purchased prized possession.

An advert from within promoting an Edgar Broughton Band album. David McPhie: "They proved to be a very popular band, with their 'rallying call' of Out Demons Out. After two bookings at the Velvet Underground, I booked them on a Chesterfield Rugby Club Outdoor Festival event, but ended up falling out with them over the running order, a sad end to their 'love affair' with Chesterfield."

This work of art was created for us by Mick Levers and John Tuck, payment for which was the loan of the car for a couple of weeks.

"The premises we found to fulfil my ambition for a very particular type of record shop was small, no more than 350sq.ft. on the ground floor, with a tiny kitchen out the back. But it had two rooms and a bathroom upstairs, so, for £10 a week (or was it £10 a month?) we had our business premises and a reasonably adequate living space.

"By this time all our friends and relatives were saying 'But it's on Newbold Road, nowhere near the town centre', and in fact it was indeed a half-mile walk from most of the prime shopping streets in the town!

"As usual, I ignored all the 'good, well intentioned, advice' as I was absolutely convinced that my 'core market' would beat

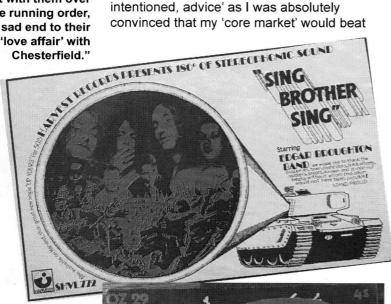

a path to our door no matter how far we were from 'civilisation', and the rent was a fraction of the town centre rate too. I was, many years later, to repeat this 'recipe' on a much larger scale, at Calver Craft Centre at Calver Bridge near Baslow in the late 1970s, Country Bookstore at Hassop Station in the 1980s, and Bookstore Brierlow Bar (latterly High Peak Bookstore and Café now that my daughter Louisa runs the business) near Buxton in 2001.

"So, with no money, we were faced with the problem of how to stock the shop with the desired 'sounds' that would be essential to attract the specialist clientele that I was aiming for. The type of music that I would be specialising in was not stocked in 'mainstream' record outlets until later.

"I successfully convinced them that we were a viable prospect to invest their trust in, and not just a couple of 'hippie dreamers'..."

"Our 'shoe-string' approach meant that our opening stock consisted of my own record collection, plus the few precious newly released 'progressive music' vinyl albums that I was able to obtain from the record companies. I successfully convinced them that we were a viable prospect to invest their trust in, and not just a couple of 'hippie dreamers' who thought it would be a good way to feed a 'hip lifestyle' or a hedonistic drug habit.

"The Led Zeppelin, Jethro Tull, King Crimson albums, and the American equivalents such as Jefferson Airplane, The Doors, Bob Dylan, etc. were by now coming 'hot off the press', many of them courtesy of the smaller specialist labels, including Chrysalis, Elektra, Virgin and Island, many of whom later became hugely successful, and almost as big and profitable as the 'majors'.

"But not to be upstaged, the traditional 'giants' themselves were quickly on the bandwagon, fighting each other to sign the new bands to their own specially created 'subsidiary' labels, EMI with Harvest, Philips with Vertigo and RCA with Neon (with whom I was soon to sign Shape of the Rain).

"This is where Velvet Underground (at the Vic) came to the rescue, as I was booking artists such as Jethro Tull, King Crimson, Fairport Convention, Family, Third Ear Band, etc. and as a consequence gained the confidence of the agents, many of whom were also connected to the record companies.

Issue 29 of OZ magazine, the one after the notorious Schoolkids OZ which provoked a lengthy obscenity trial...

"Word soon got around that there was this small specialist record shop in some anonymous northern provincial wasteland of the country, that was willing to stock and promote the recorded output of the bands that they were also promoting every week in the local club that they (we) also ran.

"Self interest soon kicked in, and I found that it became quite easy for me to open accounts with the record companies, and fill our shelves with the 'progressive and psychedelic goodies' that our clientele flocked to our 'wilderness location' to purchase.

"I think that my choices of names for shop and club (Some Kinda Mushroom and Velvet Underground) helped considerably to convince both the record companies and the booking agencies that we were the 'real deal' for the expansion of their musical takeover of the provinces.

"We lived above the shop for a couple of years, but when our first child, Louisa (to be followed shortly by Jamie) came along, the lack of space and the proximity to the business downstairs became a problem, and so we moved into a council house on Lancaster Road. With the living room upstairs now vacant we decided to serve coffee, but to call it a coffee bar was stretching credibility too far.

"With the living room upstairs now vacant we decided to serve coffee, but to call it a coffee bar was stretching credibility too far."

"As a facility for customers, many of whom by now were travelling quite a long way to visit us, it served a purpose, namely to enable them to sit in a relaxing atmosphere with friends and talk about music. However, it didn't take us long to notice that pungent aromas were emanating from this area, and of course it had become a popular place to smoke cannabis, which, although I was probably the only person within our fairly wide circle of friends who did not partake of the weed, I could not really see what harm it was doing - a situation that was soon to change!

"The St. Helena High School for Girls was around the corner from the shop, on Sheffield Road, and between classes there was always a movement of girls from the main school premises to an annexe about a hundred yards along Newbold Road, passing by the front of the shop as they did so. Some of the older ones would also call in during their lunch hour to browse the stock, or go upstairs

VIOLET MAY
(RECORD COLLECTORS CORNER)
SPECIALISTS IN DELETIONS, OPERATIC, ETC.
22 South Street, SHEFFIELD, 2
PHONE 54215 after 7 p.m.

with friends. "One day, one of the regulars told me that they had now been banned from entering the shop, and I think we received official confirmation of this via a letter from the headmistress.

"Soon after, I was warned by a friend, who had heard of a similar situation with cannabis smoking in a cafe somewhere in Yorkshire, that it was only a matter of time before we would be prosecuted for our tolerance of the situation. And so our upstairs 'coffee and cannabis facility' closed without further delay, for fear of jeopardising the whole operation!"

Richard Taylor

A semi-permanent fixture on both sides of the counter at Some Kinda Mushroom was Richard 'Rick' Taylor. He lived at Ashton Lodge on Abercrombie Street so SKM was just a short stroll away.

David McPhie: *"He was usually the first person through the door every morning, wanting to talk Marc Bolan and Tyrannosaurus Rex with anyone who would listen. He also became a Saturday assistant at some stage."*

Violet May's was a tiny record shop in Sheffield and the only outlet in the area to stock US imports. It was an essential pilgrimage for intrepid vinyl collectors in the sixties, especially before the arrival in Chesterfield of stores like SKM.

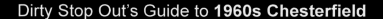

Taylor also had a big impact on the younger Richard Knight during his Mushroom days: "An appearance from Rick Taylor would top off the aura of 'cognoscenti cool'".

In fact David was so taken by Richard's unbridled enthusiasm for Bolan's Tolkienesque Tyrannosaurus Rex that he was persuaded to book the pixie folk duo for Sheffield City Hall. Unfortunately, being one of 'underground' DJ John Peel's fave raves didn't translate into national popularity and as the date approached ticket sales were flat-lining for this still cult band, forcing David to dig deep for an expensive cancellation fee.

A short time later Bolan was riding his white swan up the charts with the truncated T. Rex, and getting it on as a solid gold teen idol able to effortlessly fill a venue like the City Hall to bursting. But David bore Richard no ill feeling: "He was ahead of his time," he said.

Taylor also had a big impact on the younger Richard Knight during his Mushroom days:

"An appearance from Rick Taylor would top off the aura of 'cognoscenti cool'. I remember the day Tyrannosaurus Rex's Unicorn came out, listening to it in the shop, Rick talking me through tracks he'd already listened to an hour or so earlier.

"Always ahead of the game, Rick got to read the music press before me. He'd walk up to the newspaper wholesalers in the evening, get them fresh on a Wednesday night: *Disc* and *Music Echo, Melody Maker, NME, Record Mirror*... maybe even *Billboard*!"

Richard Martin Taylor – 30/12/51-14/02/16

Sadly, Richard died in 2016. But he is recalled fondly and warmly for his amiable eccentric ways by Philip Bargh his second cousin: "He worked in Some Kinda Mushroom record shop as well as in the trendy men's clothing boutique Mr Six in Soresby Street. Curiously the shop is now host to Maria Harris's Tallbird Records, a regular haunt of Richard's before he died.

"He grew up visiting record/music shops in the town. He was interested in music from a young age and had an almost encyclopedic knowledge of bands from the sixties, seventies and eighties. He studied and collected many music magazines of the day – and had the first ever edition of the *NME*!

"He mentioned that a popular 'high' of the time was drinking the now banned cough medicine, Phensodyl, which

Richard 'Rick' Taylor – an SKM fixture, he lived and breathed music.

led to hallucinations. He told me it was so potent he saw shapes and ghosts and ended up being chased by a ghost in the grounds of Holy Trinity Church on Sheffield Road following a particularly heavy session on the linctus. No wonder it got banned from commercial sale as a medicine!

"Richard had an interesting background growing up in the 1960s at Ashton Lodge. His grandmother, and then his parents, took in visiting theatre acts over the years as paying guests. These included stars of the day such as Roger Moore, Jimmy Jewel & Ben Warriss, Donald Pleasance, Margaret Tyzak, Val Doonican and even circus acts! Richard said the family told him they had circus animals roaming the long back garden, including lions and elephants. It seems quite unimaginable in these days of health and safety.

"On top of all the visitors passing through Ashton Lodge, he lived there with his parents, two cousins and a bachelor uncle. His Uncle George was a drummer in a swing band playing music from the thirties, forties and fifties, which had quite an influence on Richard growing up in the fifties and sixties.

"He had an almost photographic memory for music, band names and band members. He attended many music festivals where he went back stage to meet artists such as Jethro Tull and Fairport Convention. Richard often talked fondly of Fairport's bass player Ashley Hutchings (who now lives locally) and seeing him play in the late 1960s.

"He carried on his music collection until his passing. Throughout his life he amassed a very large collection of all music media and especially loved the resurgence of vinyl again in the noughties."

THE **VICTORIA BALLROOM**

CHAPTER 2

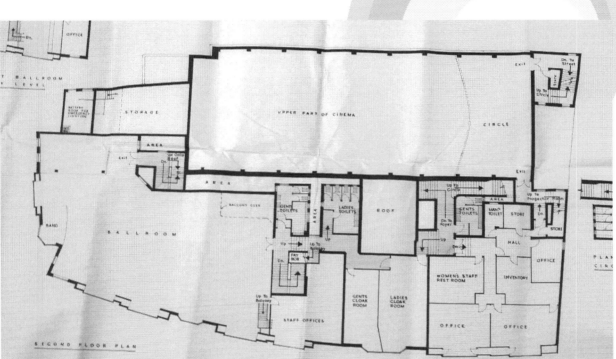

Achitectural plan of the second floor of the Vic, featuring the Ballroom and the Gaumont Cinema which stopped showing films in the mid-60s

T he grand opening of the Victoria Ballroom was on Saturday, October 5, 1929. In those days it was the dance bands that called the shots – acts such as Stan Bonsall, Harry Langstaffe, Stan Cox, Jim Lofty and Al Needham; but more on him later.

Rock 'n' roll would follow in the fifties, and in the early sixties Brit beat groups would take over. But it was in the later sixties when the venue began to provide 'progressive' music and soul and motown dance nights on different floors on the same night that the venue gained a renewed vibrancy. This was under the auspices of man-of-the-moment David McPhie, who named the live music venue The Velvet Underground.

The Velvet Underground

David McPhie explains where the name came from: "Well, the Velvet Underground (the New York band containing Lou Reed, John Cale and Nico, and sponsored by Andy Warhol) was one of the best, and most inventive, bands of the sixties, and so I deemed it appropriate to associate my new venture with such an innovative approach to music."

"Top Rank began closing uneconomic dance halls during the 1960s and into the 1970s, and the Vic was to become one of the casualties in this 'cull'. But before it was able to do so, negotiations commenced for a takeover by two brothers, one of whom had been a Top Rank manager in another part of the country.

"The Beresford Brothers, aware of my position as resident DJ, and as an independent booking agent responsible for bringing Bill Haley and Little Richard to Chesterfield, approached me to work for them as sole agent, DJ, compère and publicist.

"So, contrary to popular opinion I was not the 'proprietor' of the operation, although I did all of the booking and promoting, and indeed had carte blanche to run the show. That's the good news, the bad news was, my reward for this 'employment opportunity' was to be the princely sum of 20 pounds per week!

"I was able to claim my 10% booking fee for all contracted artist fees. These were not however substantial sums as I succeeded in obtaining the bands for very reasonable fees. I achieved this by convincing the London agents that their new, exciting bands would gain tremendous

Velvet Underground

WEST COAST AND BLUES CLUB

**Left:
A quirky Velvet Underground poster.**

exposure by being seen by sell-out northern audiences who had developed an appreciation of their music via my promotion of their records in our record shop.

"This, in retrospect, was against our own (financial) interests as I succeeded in obtaining some prime 'bargains' (Jethro Tull – £75, King Crimson – £65). Therefore my resultant 10% commission averaged about £7 per band!

"But more important than that, I thoroughly enjoyed the opportunity to book bands who were building a solid career producing vibrant, adventurous, original music with an integrity that had been previously rare."

David took a careful look at the structure of the building that the Beresfords were inheriting from Top Rank. All the groups had previously appeared, and the dancing taken place, on the professionally sprung dance floor of the designated ballroom itself, with its inset window alcoves that looked straight down into Knifesmithgate below.

There was also the popular balcony, with bar provided, from which David witnessed the 'propelling' of numerous beverages (glass attached) at times of great excitement, not to say incitement! So wasn't this the obvious place to have the club, and install the bands?

David: "Well yes, in theory, but I had always wanted to have a club where there was a small dancing area and a large 'seated in comfort to watch' area, and guess what, there was another area in the building to consider. The ballroom was on the second floor, a bingo facility on the ground floor, and in the middle a very generously sized restaurant which was available."

Once the Beresfords had been persuaded, David saw a plan forming in his mind that would become the fulfilment of a long held ambition.

David: "The first floor restaurant was to be the intimate space, with tables arranged in a 'night club' fashion around a space for the bands to set up and play; there was no raised stage, and it wasn't really necessary as everyone sat around tables and the view to the performers was uninhibited.

"For King Crimson, who opened on the first night at Velvet Underground, this was apparently their first gig outside London. After a while I began to form a reasonably friendly relationship with a couple of the agencies, and was able to trust them to recommend many bands who had, as yet, never ventured outside of the capital.

"The large second floor existing Vic Ballroom area was to host the soul and motown bands, and be a dancing space, and the DJ was to be my good friend Ken Blair.

"A large factor in the success of Velvet Underground was this 'split-level' policy, with paying customers able to move between one level and the other, although, in retrospect, I'm not quite sure just how much movement there was between the two, as the dancers (the soul and motown adherents) were not generally too interested in what was known in some circles as 'psychedelic' or 'head music', and wanted to dance all night, with an odd drink or two in between.

"Likewise, the downstairs customers generally wished to remain seated and to listen intently to the more adventurous sounds on offer. But the option was available, and that contributed to the feeling of freedom and curiosity that pervaded the atmosphere of the venue."

Because the Sheffield club options on offer were not particularly scintillating at the time the Vic attracted a substantial following from the city, in addition to Chesterfield and the surrounding towns, and most nights were completely sold out.

Rob Cupitt's association with David McPhie was far from over and in the mid-seventies he joined him at SKM on Newbold Road.

Rob: "Less than a year later we split the business, with me taking over his share of the record shop business and Dave going on to develop his bookshops in the Peak District.

"By this time the underground scene was waning and new fresh-faced kids were trying to find something away from your Floyd, Yes etc. Stuart Smith worked Saturdays and it didn't take long to pick up on his enthusiasm and popularity with this new crowd. I offered Stuart a full time job running the Mushroom and he jumped at the chance. We had maybe three years working together which we both enjoyed."

A decade later, Stuart in turn went on to replicate the Vic days of the Velvet Underground by launching the Fusion live music club in the upstairs ballroom of the former Odeon Cinema – now The Winding Wheel. Opening act the Cure. Other star turns included The Pretenders, The Specials, Doll By Doll and Punishment of Luxury.

Tripping The Light Fantastic

The Velvet Underground operated a 'light show' much of the time, and although this wasn't entirely original it was unusual for venues in the North at the time. The Round House, an old railway engine shed in Chalk Farm, London, which opened as a music and arts related venue in 1964, was by this time operating one where bands such as Pink Floyd were appearing.

David: "Rob Cupitt and Rob Haslam brought their own customised light show most nights, which added to the atmosphere and introduced a visual element to the aural soundscape."

Rob Cupitt remembers the Vic as a superb venue for discos, live bands and anyone who wanted to join the local in-crowd. Long-haired hippy types on one floor and soul/pop loving youngsters on the other.

Rob: "My time there was in the late sixties. I was just too young to catch the rock 'n' roll era. This was my time – a good time, an unbelievable time for every type of music you could wish for pouring out of radios, TVs, record shops and of course from live bands.

"The Vic had two types of follower. One the 'underground' type with their long hair, jeans and

> **"A typical Saturday night was to be in the Vic around 6.30 and set up our gear. The band would arrive soon after with the roadies humping all their gear up those dreaded Vic stairs..."**

every other word being 'man'. Or the soul/motown crowd that just happily danced the night away. You were one or the other. I chose both. At the head of all this was David McPhie, a man with his fingers in many pies when it came to the music audiences of Chesterfield.

"I had been doing a few lighting effects, commonly known as 'light shows' in those days, for a couple of local bands and the odd youth club and was asked one day by David if I would give it a go at the Vic with the live bands on a Saturday night.

"Needless to say the decision was not a hard one to make and led to myself and a good friend, Rob Haslam, having a most amazing time centred around the music scene at the Vic.

"Our set up was easy. We put up white sheets to the back of the stage prior to the band arriving and used various spotlights and projectors to create a psychedelic light show. The magic ingredient for the show was ether, obtained in rather large quantities from Greaves chemist who only once asked what it was to be used for. The projector bulbs created the heat to warm up the ether and set the show in motion.

An external shot of the Vic.

"A typical Saturday night was to be in the Vic around 6.30 and set up our gear. The band would arrive soon after with the roadies humping all their gear up those dreaded Vic stairs. The band would head straight to the dressing rooms for a little 'light refreshment' and Rob or myself would join them for a short while to get a set list and find out what they were doing that night.

"All the bands were extremely friendly and as I recall were more than satisfied with what we provided. A band named Juniors Eyes asked if we would take our light show on the road with them but life in Chesterfield seemed more interesting at the time.

"Only the memories now remain of bands such as Mott the Hoople, Family, Yes, Stone The Crows with the wonderful Maggie Bell and ultimately Pink Floyd at St James Hall. Dozens of other bands from all over the UK played our local venue the Vic, many with the odd member who went on to fame and fortune in future years.

"A wonderful time, an amazing venue and an audience of locals who truly knew their music. It was my pleasure to be part of it all."

Richard Knight recalls listening cross-legged and entranced to the Third Ear Band at the Velvet Underground: "I was 14 years old in my greatcoat and white tennis shoes, while the skinheads next door were doing a blood curdling Moonstomp. Some skins stood at the door shouting 'Ma-gics' – meaning we looked like something from Middle Earth – and generally putting a very different vibe into play. I'd read in *Peace News* that the Third Ear Band could transport you into a different time dimension if you let the music take you.

"I stared at the psychedelic oil-wheel light show and attempted transportation but I just couldn't help thinking about whether I could get to the 31 bus on Elder Way without getting smacked!"

Pink Floyd played St James' Hall promoting their second (and largely Syd-less) album Saucerful of Secrets.

Pink Floyd

St James Hall, Chesterfield, England

March 27 1969

Bill Haley was at the Vic in 1968, booked by David McPhie. Haley was enjoying a 'second wind' after his fifties heyday.

The Church Fête

As you will later learn, your author gained his first experience of live performance through the package tours that visited the ABC Cinema. But before that:

Pete Dodd: "As if by magic, as the package tours of the early to mid-sixties dwindled, a burgeoning local live scene seemed to be establishing itself – now was the time for a young man to move on to the 'proper gig'. The first one I wanted to attend was The Nice at the Vic Ballroom. Like the Small Faces they were an Immediate label act and I had a copy of their instrumental version of Leonard Bernstein's *America* from *West Side Story* with Keith Emerson on organ and Davey O'List on some fairly abstract guitar.

"That afternoon I had, untypically, been running a stall at a fête in Old Brampton churchyard. A girl on the neighbouring stall invited me to join her at Springbank Youth Club in Chesterfield that evening. Naively thinking there might be more to it than there was, and favouring an opportunity to shed a smidgen of light on the conundrum of what happens when a man loves a woman, I ditched a chance to catch a proper gig.

"Instead, I popped along to the youth club with a friend and spent a few moments talking to her and, disappointingly, her boyfriend before we made our excuses and left – alas too late to catch up with The Nice, and none the wiser about affairs of the heart.

"So I can't remember the first show I witnessed

at David McPhie's Velvet Underground (and at that time I didn't understand the hip New York band reference either). But it must have been soon after the Nice gig. Bands I did see included Free, Yes, Stone the Crows, Blodwyn Pig, East of Eden, Third Ear Band and the Edgar Broughton Band. And of course Chesterfield's own Shape of the Rain quite a few times in support of the visiting headliners. If you showed me a list, there would probably be more. Principal Edwards Magic Theatre? Missed them twice, I think. The Amazing Blondel?
Couldn't tell ya."

Valuable prep time

"Most of these gigs I attended with my classmate Tom Bailey and we formulated a number of procedures to enhance the experience:
1. Go to the off-licence on the newly arrived and still under construction Loundsley Green estate late in the afternoon and buy a pint of draught sherry in a plastic bottle (no ID in those days).
2. Knock it back down by the Holme Brook river.
3. Drift into town as said tincture takes effect.
4. Hang around the Vic Veranda to see if the band or crew shows up in a van.
5. If they do, ask if they would like a hand with the gear. If they say yes, carry some stuff upstairs and lurk around in dark corners in assumed roadie mode until punters start arriving (sorry David McPhie!). Result: enough cash in pocket for another drink or two.

"We probably pulled free entry off only a couple of times, but this early arrival policy meant you sort of met the occasional musician and got to know the psychedelic light show supremos Rob Cupitt and Rob Haslam who just about tolerated us wet-behind-the-ears whipper-snappers. We were grown-ups at last."

Uptown Top Ranking

Before the advent of the McPhie years at the Vic, many of the leading beat groups of the early to mid-sixties came to town under the Top Rank banner.

Eileen Marriott remembers the groups and the dancing fondly: "Every Saturday I would wake up excited by the prospect of going to the Vic Saturday and Sunday. First I had to do my Saturday job at the Co-op for the money to go out with as I was still in the 6th form at St. Helena School. Went home to get ready – I didn't have many outfits so I suppose we wore the same things week in week out. I do remember a green cord mini skirt with yellow skinny rib polo neck jumper and cheap white boots (my friend had a red skirt and white jumper).

"Veronica Sanderson was my main dance 'partner' always there until she moved to London to be a nanny. Another good friend

was lovely Liz Meakin who sadly died aged 22 from lung cancer. I still carried on going to the Vic and was soon dancing with friends Maureen Edwards, Pat Horton and Sandra Robson. "So it was under the Vic veranda and up the two flights of stairs to the dance hall. The best place in Chesterfield, or so we thought! Usually David Oxley would be around. He was the manager and we thought he was quite old, but looking back he must have been about 30! I think it cost about 4/6d to go in on a normal weekend, but we got in for free whenever we could.

Above: Posters for Shape of the Rain

Shape of the Rain were managed by David McPhie and often appeared as the support act to visiting groups at the Vic. Their album on Neon/RCA, Riley, Riley, Wood and Waggett (featuring 100% original material) was, according to McPhie, a 'disappointment' as the production did not reflect their 'live' sound.

THE RANK ORGANISATION
TOP RANK DANCING DIVISION 343
Membership No.
TOP RANK SUNDAY DANCING CLUB

Victoria Ballroom Chesterfield
I have read the club rules as exhibited on the club premises and
hereby undertake to abide by them and conform to, such rules
as existing or as hereafter amended.
Membership will be forfeited if improper use is made of this
card. In the event of this card being lost it may be replaced on
application to the Manager.

Signed B. Newton   Date 5/9/65.
(Member's Signature)
This card is not transferable. It must be presented for admittance
and produced on demand.   F.4396—1/63

A group of Queen's Head drinkers step outside for a breath of fresh air and a photo opportunity.

"There was always a row of chairs about 12ft away from the stage for people to sit and watch the group. But no, not us, we danced

> **"There was always a row of chairs about 12ft away from the stage for people to sit and watch the group. But no, not us, we danced in front like go-go dancers!"**

in front like go-go dancers! Well that's what we thought we looked like! This is what we did all night, dance and chat to the bands. We never had a drink, we thrived on the adrenalin!

"The place was also open Monday and Thursday, just with records and sometimes competitions. We didn't go too often, no money, but I remember one time they'd got a silhouette shape of a big busty woman. There was a prize was for the person who could fit the shape. Of course no-one ever would dare try it, so we did, and won a load of goodies.

"Some of the bands who came were quite famous and usually played in the week. Then proper barriers were put round the stage in case of mobbing. We were a bit more sophisticated (we thought) than that.

A few of the bigger bands I remember were – The Kinks (I had a lovely kiss from Dave Davies), The Hollies (still love their music), Wayne Fontana, The

Who (Keith Moon asked me if I was Mary Poppins! Don't ask!!), Nashville Teens, The Merseys (my favourite band, when they were the Merseybeats and Aaron Williams was with them), Dave Dee, Dozy, Beaky, Mick and Titch, and Small Faces (though I wasn't too keen on them in those days).

"I also remember a band from Birmingham called The In Between. They did okay for themselves after they changed their name to Slade!!

"Can't remember much about any other bands – it's 50 years ago – but according to my 1966 diary we saw Pinkerton's Assorted Colours, Mama's Darlings, Ian Landon and the Burnettes, R&B Inc, Cheetahs, Country Gents, Fitz 'n' Startz, Cimerons, Hells Bells, Paddy Klaus and Gibson, Jimmy Winston's Reflections, James Royal and the Hawks, The Group, The Warriors, Measles, Emeralds, The Breed, Ian Edwards and the Zodiacs, Wynder K Frogg, Attack, Sons and Lovers, The Knack, Mike Ray and the Condors, Tiffany's Thoughts, Carnaby, and Wednesday's Child, to name but a few. Most of them faded into oblivion. But what a lot of good times with happy, happy memories."

Jazz – Delicious Hot, Disgusting Cold

The original purpose of the Victoria Ballroom was for big bands and dancing. Local outfits were playing tunes and arrangements derived from the big international bands of the time; names like Americans Glenn Miller and Benny Goodman, and Britons Ambrose and Lew Stone. And Al Needham represented the 'last bastion' of the genre in the town, co-existing well into the sixties despite the increasing profile of the new kids on the block, rock 'n' roll and the beat groups.

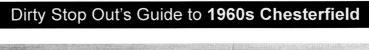

US imports Bowling Alleys were accompanied by Skating Rinks. Sheffield's Silver Blades arrived in 1965, courtesy of Mecca.

The celebrated Chesterfield trumpet player was the band leader at the venue for much of the era and adapted to the seismic changes in musical style with the rise of beat music, Beatles-charged pop hysteria and more.

Chesterfield offered a range of dance nights with resident bands. The nearby Co-Op rooms was popular.

Jack Fazackerley's Band had been keeping the masses entertained in the years leading up to the 1960s. There was also St James Hall (better known as 'Jimmys') on Vicar Lane – often with Stan Bonsall and his band keeping people entertained. And there was also Jim Lofty's band at the Odeon around the period.

Top Rank ran the Victoria Ballroom on Monday and Saturday nights – the other nights of the week were for private hire and very popular.

Though it was a thrill for Al Needham to be given the job of band leader it came at a price. The Stan Cox Orchestra had been the resident band for 29 years and Al Needham's father was a member.

Al Needham: "Rank rang me up and at that point I was playing at the Palais in Nottingham. They offered me the Victoria Ballroom job. The hardest part was having to tell my father that I was taking over as band leader and trumpet player. I was 27 at that point."

Needham was already no stranger to the band he was replacing: "I did my first big show with Stan Cox's band at the age of 18. I played with them when my father was off."

"We were just finishing off the dance band days of ballroom. Things were moving into pops. We had to start playing the likes of *It's Not Unusual* by Tom Jones...."

Needham performed at the 500 capacity Victoria Ballroom through much of the 1960s – at the rank nights and scores of private functions. He remembers the big changes in music and enjoyed being a part of the pop explosion of the era.

Al: "We were just finishing off the dance band days of ballroom. Things were moving into pops. We had to start playing the likes of *It's Not Unusual* by Tom Jones. Things were changing fast. It was marvellous."

Al Needham – one of the last of the great bandleaders.

He moved from the Victoria Ballroom to take a residency at Sheffield City Hall in 1967. It was the end of an era for nightlife in Chesterfield. But he was decades from retiring – that only came very recently.

He went on to perform at Sheffield's popular Hofbrauhaus in the 1970s, became a regular on TV and even had his own dedicated civic reception in Chesterfield in 1993 to honour his services to music and the town. He also did a nine year stint at Sheffield City Hall. It was quite

a career for the Chesterfield lad who started playing at eight years old and fondly remembers disappearing off to the nearby King and Miller pub for a swift drink with the rest of the band between spots at the Victoria Ballroom in the sixties.

Though Victoria Ballroom nights of the era are a distant memory one thing did survive: "There was a glass revolving door at the entrance that you went through when you paid. It finished up at The Gate Inn at Cutthorpe years later."

The King and Miller

One of Al Needham's favourite haunts, as mentioned above, was the King and Miller pub, which was across the road from the Vic where Primark now stands.

Susan Chaudhri (then Metcalf) now a resident of Chicago in the US and working for the Indo-American Center grew up in the King and Miller.

Susan: "I left Chesterfield in 1963 aged 18. My dad died the previous year and he was very strict about under age drinking so I can't remember ever being in the bars during opening hours.

"It was a very popular pub in those days though. There were five bars between Knifesmithgate and the Market Place. The Saloon Bar and the King and Miller Bar were on Knifesmithgate, and the one half way down the yard was the Snack Bar,

The Berni Inn steakhouse next to the Queen's Head pub, was an ideal town centre location for a romantic meal for two.

"I think the next one was called the Top Bar and it was TP Woods at the market end and the yard. It was

a Mansfield pub and only sold Mansfield Ales. The Golden Fleece was Tetleys. The K&M was demolished in 1967.

Nearby Glumangate boasted three popular pubs in the sixties – The Corner House (later The Manhattan and now a Thai restaurant), The Gardener's Arms (now a financial advisers) and the Queen's Head Hotel (quite recently a fairly short-lived lap dancing club and currently (2018) a Greek restaurant).

The Queen's Head which shared its premises with the Berni Inn steakhouse, where many young couples would enjoy their first 'proper' meal out (and possibly a black coffee in a wine glass with thick cream floating on top looking like a small Guinness), was tolerant of underage drinkers and some recreational drug usage. It was understandably very popular and eventually closed down presumably for exactly the same reasons it was so popular.

HUDSONS -
A FAMILY BUSINESS

Left: Setting up the new Hudsons shop with staff member Roger Pattison, also a highly regarded local guitarist of the time.

I f David McPhie was the hippy entrepreneur of the time, Keith Hudson was the establishment figure – part of a Chesterfield family music retail empire whose roots stretched back to the beginning of the 20th Century.

Traditionally Hudsons was a supplier of pianos, organs, orchestral instruments and sheet music, at various locations around the town, but by the time Keith took the reins the cultural revolution that was the 1960s was getting underway.

Keith: "In the sixties, most of my memories are of working in the musical instrument department of Hudsons. I worked there from about 1962, and was at the piano shop between 1960/62. From about 1962 the number of local bands just grew and grew.

"Hudsons had the small shop on the outside of the Market Hall, opposite the old main post office where they sold musical instruments and music. The basement of the shop was the LP record department, and the stall inside the Market Hall was very busy with mainly singles – which is where the famous David McPhie began his career in records.

"At weekends particularly the instrument shop used to be packed and jammed particularly for guitar, amp, PA and drum sales. How we packed it into such a small shop I will never know."

Keith notes there were many bands all over the Chesterfield and North Derbyshire area, but in Matlock there seemed to be one from nearly every street! As a result he delivered gear to Matlock, Darley Dale and Bakewell on a regular basis, and made many friends there.

Keith: "I remember going to one group practice session to take some equipment over for them to try out. The practice room was in the basement of an old spa building in Matlock Bath. The building was virtually derelict, although it has been 'restored' and is still there.

"The lighting was a couple of bare bulbs, strung up, and the inside was strewn with all sorts of debris.

"At the back of the basement there was another big room where a big waterfall with water from the hills behind cascaded through and out below, accompanied by a loud roaring sound. All quite surreal!"

Rarities

In 1963 Keith took an order from a customer for a Gibson ES175 – a full-bodied cutaway electric guitar, at the time and since, mainly used in jazz. The customer then cancelled the order, and the guitar was put in stock and hung on the wall for two to three years.

Keith: "Whilst we were selling slim bodied Gibsons and Gretsches and solid bodied Fender Strats, nobody wanted it. We couldn't give it away. It was priced at £140! Eventually it was sold – we were pleased to have found it a good home. What would it be worth today – a vintage Gibson from the early sixties: £2,000/£3,000?

"We also used to sell a lot of Hofner guitars – mainly electrics. These were Coloramas, Galaxies, Verithins and Violin Basses – plus a small number of acoustic Presidents. They were attractively styled and good instruments for a reasonable price.

"Drums were Premier, Olympic and Ludwig. I remember working late on a Friday night in the small front window of the Market Hall shop to display a new Ludwig oyster finish kit, which had just been delivered. I spent ages getting everything just right with the kit as the centrepiece of the display, with guitars and various other equipment carefully placed. The kit looked fabulous.

"We opened at nine on the Saturday morning. At five past one of our drummers came in. "The kit in the window," he said breathlessly, "I'll have it." You could hardly blame him. A Ludwig oyster finish kit at the time was cool. But bye-bye shop window display!"

All That Jazz

Keith loved his business and keeping astride the latest musical developments on the local live scene was part of the fun:

"Sheffield City Hall was (and is) always a great venue for bands, jazz and classical. July 1964 saw a memorable concert. Chuck Berry headlined, but the bill also featured Carl Perkins, the Nashville Teens and the Animals. The Animals had only just released 'House of the Rising Sun' and I think it charted the week of the concert. Eric Burdon, Alan Price and Chas Chandler all looked about 15! A great night.

"Most of my music nights there were jazz. The early and mid-sixties were a fantastic period for tours by the American bands and jazz 'greats'. Brubeck, Basie, Dizzy Gillespie, Woody Herman, Ella Fitzgerald, Jimmy Giuffre, Charlie Byrd. There were also several 'Jazz at the Philharmonic' tours which came to Sheffield – with Oscar Peterson,

"Most of my music nights there were jazz. The early and mid-sixties were a fantastic period for tours by the American bands and jazz 'greats'".

Roy Eldridge, Sonny Stitt and many more.

"One of my best nights was seeing Erroll Garner around 1965 – but that was in Leicester at the De Montfort Hall. It had a wooden floor which really rocked as things got cranked up. Garner said later to one of our record reps, whose job it was to chauffeur him around on some of the UK tours, that the Leicester gig was the best.

"I also saw Duke Ellington at a cinema in the Square in Nottingham city centre. I went there by train, and just before I had to leave early to catch the last train home they started to play "Diminuendo and Crescendo in Blue", which is a cracking piece of rocking big band jazz, featuring Paul Gonzalvez.

"I managed to hear most of it before making a dash for it. I must have broken the world record for running between Nottingham Square and the railway station.

Back at the City Hall, in 1965 I think, I saw Thelonious Monk. This was another memorable night, musically and for his drinking in between choruses. What was disappointing, looking back, was that the hall was only about one third full – seems odd now for the visit of such a towering jazz icon."

Silly Stories

Keith has no shortage of anecdotes from the period: "Here are some silly tales from the sixties. Two teenage lads were looking in the back window (inside the Market Hall), which displayed musical stuff. This could be a real mixture, including small items like harmonicas, ocarinas, jaws harps, etc. We would get asked for all sorts of strange things which had nothing to do with music, such as darts, swords, etc.

"Roy Stafford, who could have a dry wit, gave a regular reply to these strange requests, and when

Below: Keith just before his town centre Record and Tape Centre closed its doors for the final time.

one of the two lads asked for something non-musical he used his usual reply. "No, we haven't got any of those, but we've got a second-hand lighthouse." The lad thought for a minute, then went to speak to his mate who was outside, still looking in the window.

"After a minute or so he came back into the shop and said to Roy, quite seriously, "Can we see it please?" Roy was probably quite speechless, but he never used that reply again!

"Bob Johnson used to help on the record stall inside the Market Hall on Saturdays. A lady asked him "Have you got *Great Balls of Fire*?" "I'm not the devil, madam," Bob replied.

"A teenage girl called Wanda worked for Hudsons in the musical shop for several months. She was very good, and greeted the customers in a very pleasant way. On her first day at work, it was a very hot summer Saturday afternoon. A 'senior' lady came in and sat down on a stool, which was in the shop.

"..We wanted bright red electric guitars, loud amplifiers, sparkly drum kits and everything that went with it – the music, the clothes, the scene.

"It's so hot today, isn't it?" she said to Wanda. "Yes it is", Wanda replied. "Can I have my feet done please?" asked the lady. Wanda immediately cracked out laughing, not realising that we were the next door shop to Dr Scholl's foot care place. The lady was rather cross and trooped off next door to relieve her feet.

"Bob Johnson was Hudsons piano technician and tuner for many years. When he needed extra assistance, possibly with lifting pianos or working on instruments, one of the staff at the Market Hall shop would go out with him. On one occasion he asked to borrow a number of extra tools and equipment, which were at the Market Hall workshop.

"He drove down from the Saltergate piano shop where he had been working and parked his green Mini Van outside the shop, just to one side. He asked Jack Taylor, who was going with him, to load up all the extra tools whilst he went into the basement to check on something.

"He came back up the stairs and shouted to Jack: "Ready?" "Yes," said Jack, and they went out of the shop door. Bob turned left to where he had parked the van. Jack turned right to an identical green minivan in which he had loaded all the equipment.

"They got all the gear out of the 'wrong' van and put it in ours just in time. Only a minute or so after they had driven off the driver of the other van came out of the post office and drove off!"

Bright Red Guitars

As a teenager fresh out of school with no qualifications but an unquenchable passion for music, Paul Hobday was pleased as punch when he landed himself a job at Hudsons.

Paul: "In 1969 when I worked there, Hudsons Music wasn't just a shop – it was the hub of the music scene in Chesterfield and its environs.

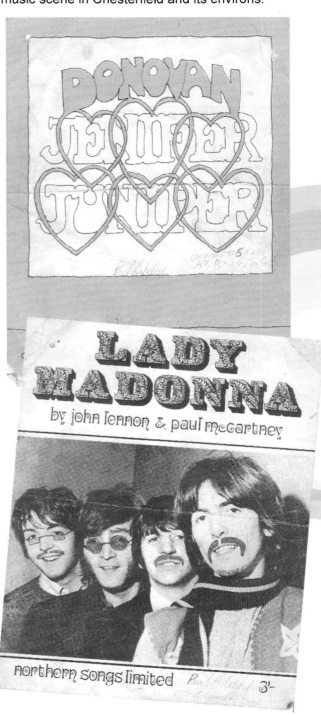

Two examples of sheet music bought from Hudsons in the 1960s. The Lady Madonna one was skilfully embellished(!) at the time by its owner Paul Hobday who also worked for Hudsons in the late sixties.

"The long history of this family business (established 1907) was still very much in evidence. 'Old' Mr Hudson (as we referred to him) looked after the piano department and his wife specialised in sheet music and classical records. All very Victorian, unchanged and formal.

"But times were changing, and my generation had little admiration for the skills of a French polisher, piano tuner or any of that 'old' stuff. Hell no, we wanted bright red electric guitars, loud amplifiers, sparkly drum kits and everything that went with it – the music, the clothes, the scene.

"To their immense credit, Mr and Mrs Hudson recognised this and gave their son Keith free rein to develop the retail side of the business. Mr Hudson built a piano showroom on the outskirts of town, with an excellent workshop and tuition rooms above, and Mrs Hudson remained in the town shop where she could run her part of the business and generally keep an eye on things.

"Saturdays in the shop were very busy. Kids would come in and hang around, looking at all the fabulous guitars. Some guys would ask to try a guitar and then make the most awful racket..."

"My job was to learn how to fix guitars and amplifiers, and to work in the shop on Saturdays. This was absolute paradise for me because I was totally obsessed with learning to play the guitar, and here I was working among some top notch players, all of whom were more than happy to coach me.

"The only fly in the ointment was that after a short while my mentor Dave and I were sent to the new workshops on the edge of town – which meant we were under the scrutiny of 'old' Mr Hudson, who had little patience with young noisy guitar players.

"Dave was a really good rock guitar player, and every day I'd ask him to show me some new things to learn. Upstairs in the new building also housed the teaching rooms and in particular, that of Fred Baker who taught classical guitar. He would send me to the shop to buy his tobacco and regularly ask if there was "any chance of a cuppa?"

"More importantly for me, Fred would come by when I was practising and say: 'Look if you must play that rubbish, at least play it properly. Sit up. You lean over the guitar, don't lean the guitar toward you.

When he's not playing and teaching bass, Fred T. Baker sells his eggs at the Neptune Beer Emporium.

Fingers parallel to the frets.' – and I'd soak all of this up.

"Every Saturday, I'd work in the shop with a terrific jazz player called Pat. He had a Gretsch White Falcon – possibly the most expensive electric guitar available back then. So, I would show Pat my latest learnings and Pat would say "that's great, so let's think about those chords you're playing – suppose we do this? And change that to this?" etc – and I'd soak that up too. Fifty years later I'm still grateful to Dave, Pat and Fred. (Editor's note: Fred Baker's son Fred Thelonious Baker (born June 4, 1960) is a force to be reckoned with in Chesterfield today. The guitarist and bassist is celebrated for his work with ex-Hatfield and the North guitarist the late Phil Miller in the Canterbury scene band In Cahoots. When he's not teaching at Birmingham Conservatoire or the University of Huddersfield, Fred can often be spotted performing around town. He played a tremendous memorial concert for his In Cahoots cohort Miller at the Neptune Beer Emporium in 2018, where his duck and chicken eggs are also on sale. The same year he performed a similar tribute at the 50th Stainsby Festival.)

"Saturdays in the shop were very busy. Kids would come in and hang around, looking at all the fabulous guitars. Some guys would ask to try a guitar and then make the most awful racket, one guy in particular came in every Saturday and sat playing the same Gretsch Tennessean guitar for an hour or more – thankfully he was a good player!

"None of this bothered Keith at all, he knew that these guys would buy from Hudsons when they could, and he operated (astonishing today) his own credit system where the customer had a paying in book, and the shop had a master ledger. By not chucking the kids out, Keith got to know them, and knew who to trust by the time they left school, got a job, and wanted to buy a guitar.

"Saturday was also the day when all the local band members came into the shop clutching their paying in books – often paying just five shillings (25p) or so off their instrument. I think there was an agreed regular amount, but Keith was incredibly kind and when a customer was having a hard time paying, he'd always allow them to pay less for a while – the stipulation being that they must pay something each week.

"I was able to buy a Fender Telecaster in this way, and even when I moved away to Devon I would send postal orders to Keith every week until it was paid off. It was certainly a different world back then. Opposite the shop there was (and still is) a very busy market. Mrs Hudson would regularly walk through it clutching canvas bank bags with the shop takings in them. They had the name of the bank printed on them, so it was obvious what they were, but she insisted there was no risk and ignored all warnings.

"Just before Christmas 1970, when we were really busy, I got a really bad cold and 'went sick' on a Saturday. I asked my landlady to phone in for me. Wrapped up in scarves I ventured out to the chemists and back, then retired to bed for the weekend. Unbeknown to me, my landlady forgot to make the phone call, and 'old' Mr Hudson had seen me on my trip to the chemist. Hence, the moment I arrived all recovered on Monday, I got a rocket and was given my cards. 'Old' Mr Hudson was quite scary, and he was in no mood to hear my side of the story. I was devastated.

"Looking back, I've no doubt that Mr H was aware that I probably spent more time playing guitars than fixing them and was glad of an excuse to dispense with my services. I think Keith was sad to see me go, but understandably had to accept his father's decision. Ever the gentlemen, Keith remained just as friendly after I left.

Ten years ago, I walked into Hudson's Music for the first time in 40 years. Astonishingly, Keith immediately recognised me and greeted me by name – and he was exactly as I had remembered him; kind, courteous, and good company.

Saturday Girl

Iris Allen (now Gaunt) found her first Saturday job at Woolworths, but was lucky enough, by her own reckoning, to move to Hudsons.

Iris Allen (now Gaunt).

Iris: "Life really began for me when I started working for the Hudson family on the stall in the Market Hall. As a Saturday girl I got to know about every musical event in the area.

"On Tuesday evenings we gathered at an informal folk event in a small upstairs room in the Yellow Lion on Saltergate.

"On Friday folk was at the now demolished Queen's Park Hotel on Markham Road where we saw Ralph McTell and Lindisfarne amongst others.

"The hub of my social life was without doubt the Market Hotel, just a stone's throw from the Hudsons shop. There was a Dansett record player at the back of the pub where you chose a disc and put it on. I had the honour of choosing three singles every Saturday – you had me to thank if the music was not to your liking!

"In the summer of 1969 the record reps told us that there was a rumour the Rolling Stones would be playing a free concert at Hyde Park. We really didn't think it would happen – but happen it did. We sat in the sunshine under the trees watching the butterflies fly.

"The following year reps from EMI and Decca gave us several tickets for the Bob Dylan concert on the Isle of White. I spent two days sitting in a field with friends lapping up all the music.

"My very happy memories from those times are down to the Hudson family – who were excellent employers – and the group of friends I met while working there. We are still good friends and stay in touch. Life has been good to me and I have always met wonderful people."

Mick Jagger releases butterflies in memory of Brian Jones at Hyde Park in 1969

Uncle Alf

John Ashforth was a Hudsons shopper who would drool over the guitars and made his first vinyl purchases there.

John: "I bought my first single, *Telstar* by the Tornados, and my first album, *Music From Big Pink* by the Band, from their stall in the market hall.

"I had a special connection with Hudsons as my Uncle Alf worked in the musical instrument department. Musician, artist and philosopher, he was my role model and quiet, almost silent mentor. He played violin, taught classical guitar and also worked as a freelance illustrator/graphic artist. I had my first guitar lessons with him on his Pedersen classical.

"Music was strong in our family. Grandad had been a violin teacher and his three sons all played instruments semi-professionally. His three daughters, including my mother, were all competent singers. Some of my most cherished early memories are hearing my three uncles play, especially Uncle Jack belting out 12th Street Rag on the harmonica.

"He used to transpose Mozart for the chromatic harmonica and play in his greenhouse. He knew that plants enjoyed classical music decades before the Findhorn Community and scientists found out. His tomatoes were the best in the village.

"Uncle Doug played saxophone in a dance band. I worked at the violin

Bags of fun for music lovers.

for a few years and although I loved classical music I wasn't inspired enough to give the commitment it demanded."

A Basilica of Wonders

Richard Knight: "Records became a big part of my world. They seemed to be everywhere. Furniture shops sold records. Eyres department store sold records. Buy a gramophone, buy some records.

"Hudsons sold records at the far end of The Market Hall. The whole building was a basilica of wonders; smell of sawdust, vegetables, darkness, light coming from somewhere above, music and noise. I could hardly see over the counter when I bought my first singles there. *For Your Love* by The Yardbirds, *Gloria* by Them, *Rosalyn* by Pretty Things.

"Later, I got to about 12 and discovered Bob Dylan singles in the plywood boxes on the semi circular stall. *Got From a Buick 6/Positively 4th Street* and *Highway 61/Can You Please Crawl Out Your Window*.

"Vibes from the second hand magazine stand and smells of Halva, Polish sausage and cheesecake from the deli. And Pez dispensers."

Starting As You Mean To Continue

David McPhie's Some Kinda Mushroom wasn't a bolt out of the blue. David paid his dues working at Hudsons in the early 1960s learning the craft of the record retailer.

David: "Record stores have been an integral part of the retail profile of many towns and cities in America and Britain since the early 1900s, and occasionally share shop space with a musical instrument department. This was indeed the model that was so successful for the late lamented Hudsons in the Market Hall in Chesterfield for so many years.

"I worked at Hudsons for a few years and was latterly the buyer in the singles department, which was in the interior of the Market Hall, immediately opposite the back door of the musical instrument shop that fronted onto the main road opposite the Post Office.

"Margaret Hudson (one half of the senior partnership of Stanley and Margaret Hudson) was my immediate 'boss', and son Keith was in charge of the musical instrument department and the sheet music section in the main shop, which also had a basement. His father Stanley looked after the piano shop on Saltergate.

"After a few months Margaret handed over the buying duties for the 7" '45s' to me. This was a job that I enjoyed, but with some reservations, as the bulk of the sales were of course 'Top Fifty Pop', and some of the Number Ones in particular, occasionally spending more than ten weeks in the charts, were (to put it mildly) excruciating to have to listen to when one was required to play them up to perhaps 50 times a day on a busy Saturday.

"Certain titles can still stir nightmares. Ones that come to mind include the Tornados *Telstar*, Del Shannon's *Swiss Maid,* Dave Clark's *Glad All Over*, Ken Dodd's *Tears*, and anything and everything by Gerry and the Pacemakers, Herman's Hermits, Freddie and the Dreamers and Engelbert Humperdinck

"Consolation was however to be found in the company of some of my working colleagues. Margaret's sister Doris was 'an old hand' on the stall, with many years' experience and a fund of entertaining stories about the early years before rock 'n' roll. But she has now sadly passed away, as have also both senior Hudsons, Stanley and Margaret.

"Also working alongside me when I first started were Jack Taylor and Reg Darby, eventually to be superceded by Andrew Peppitt, soon to become the Blueberries guitarist, and Mick Twelves, a

"Certain titles can still stir nightmares. Ones that come to mind include the Tornados Telstar, Del Shannon's Swiss Maid, Dave Clark's Glad All Over, Ken Dodd's Tears, and anything and everything by Gerry and the Pacemakers, Herman's Hermits, Freddie and the Dreamers and Engelbert Humperdinck."

member of both the Richard Jackson Blues Band and King Mob Echo, and recently (via many more outfits over the years) bass guitarist with The Pitz.

"Latterly we were joined by Joyce Orton, becoming, by default, the (only slightly) elder stateswoman and a stabilising influence on the by now otherwise all male, all music obsessed, staff on the Market Hall stall side of the establishment.

"One of the welcome 'diversions' from the 'Top Fifty Chart Music' sales that were the 'bread and butter' of the singles stall, was my encouragement of the small local population of Jamaicans, first and second generation immigrants who were looking for the blue beat and ska records by Jamaican bands and solo artists that were released on the Blue Beat label in the first half of the sixties.

"I picked up the general idea of what constituted a good, danceable, blue beat record from one of the older Jamaican residents, Fergus, who would buy anything up to a dozen records a week if he was in the mood. He would then spread the word and another dozen or so of his friends would visit me asking for the same sounds. I spent quite a lot of time looking for the best blue beat and ska singles, and our sales became quite respectable.

"However, there was a problem, and that was the tendency of most of the Jamaicans to want to listen to at least an additional dozen or so records for every one that they bought, thus usually spending a minimum of an hour or so over a purchase of two or three discs, which could present a problem if we were short staffed during the week and there were other customers wanting my attention too.

"This did not escape the ever vigilant Margaret Hudson who would give me a 'proprietorial glare' from behind the counter in the main shop if my attendance on the requirements of Fergus or his friends became too lengthy.

"The real saving grace however, and the reason that I was able to retain some semblance of sanity amidst the barrage of 'throwaway pop' that was the prevalent 'sound of the times' was the advent of the blues and soul influenced British Beat groups, foremost of course being The Beatles and Rolling Stones, followed by the Kinks, Animals, Spencer Davis, Them, Yardbirds, Small Faces, Manfred Mann, etc... plus some early examples of the equally exciting folk and blues influenced bands emerging from the West Coast of America.

"These did however seem to be very much the exception, and it is often forgotten that the early sixties was not the 'golden musical era' that we may recall. That came in the late sixties with the arrival of Bob Dylan, Jefferson Airplane, The Doors, Country Joe and the Fish, Grateful Dead, etc. and the flowering of the 'hippie' and alternative cultural movements that carried forward into the first few years of the 1970s. And this musical 'signpost' was the catalyst for my decision to leave the relative security of Hudsons and take the step into the unknown that was self employment and Some Kinda Mushroom.

The Queen's Park Hotel. Now demolished but once home to the folk club.

14552   **1963 WITH GEORGE MARTIN**

14553   **1964**

353   **1964**

3726   **1969**

1992 / 30245

© EMI RECORDS UK / APPLE CORPS LTD.

THE BEATLES

Apple

PARLOPHONE

Four poses from the Fab Four in the sixties.

THE BEATLES - THE SHEFFIELD CONNECTION

Sheffield's relationship with the Beatles went far deeper than the string of concerts the band performed there between 1963 and 1965.

The city was actually home to the mother of Brian Epstein, the band's mercurial manager who ended up nearly as famous as the band members themselves.

Known as Queenie by most, 18-year-old Malka (Hebrew for 'Queen'), married 29-year-old Harry Epstein at the Synagogue, Wilson Road, Sheffield 11, in 1933. Her father, Louis Hyman, owned the Sheffield Cabinet Company. Their most famous item, the Clarendon bedroom suite, is quite a collectors' item now by all accounts.

> **"There's no doubt it was this concert that elevated promoter Peter Stringfellow into a different league from his contemporaries. It's hard to think that \the whole thing was co-ordinated from his local phone box."**

The Beatles' show at the Azena Ballroom in Gleadless (then still part of North Derbyshire until boundary changes a year or two later) has taken on almost mythical status. There's no doubt it was this concert that elevated promoter Peter Stringfellow into a different league from his contemporaries. It's hard to

think that the whole thing was co-ordinated from his local phone box.

The gig was originally booked for the home of Peter Stringfellow's Black Cat Club, St Aiden's Hall, but as the band's career hit a vertical trajectory in the spring of 1963, so did ticket sales.

With 2,000 tickets sold Stringfellow had no option but to find a bigger venue. He tried for the Mecca dance hall but failed and opted for the Azena.

It was a scene of total chaos at the event with hundreds turning up without tickets – windows were smashed and the fire doors mysteriously opened.

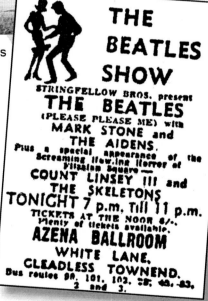

THE BEATLES SHOW
STRINGFELLOW BROS. present
THE BEATLES
(PLEASE PLEASE ME) with
MARK STONE and
THE AIDENS.
Plus a special appearance of the
Screaming Howling Horror of
Filipino Square—
COUNT LINSEY III and
THE SKELETONS
TONIGHT 7 p.m. Till 11 p.m.
TICKETS AT THE DOOR 6/-.
Plenty of tickets available.
AZENA BALLROOM
WHITE LANE,
GLEADLESS TOWNEND.
Bus routes 9A, 101, 102, 28, 40, 83, 3 and 3.

The Beatles' infamous gig at the Azena Club in Gleadless has taken on almost mythical status and helped establish promoter Peter Stringfellow's career.

> ***Paul Cooper***: *"I can still remember the night vividly. I don't think Gleadless has ever seen an event quite like it! I remember paying 6s 6d for a ticket on the black market outside the venue, I think the original price was 5s 6d.*
> *"Someone managed to open the Azena fire door and hundreds poured in till the police came in and somehow restored order. It was absolute bedlam."*

Queenie Epstein, Brian's mum, was a Sheffield lass.

John Firminger: " Like many hundreds of others who went to see The Beatles at the Azena in Gleadless, I couldn't get in and had to console myself by nipping over the hill to Frecheville Community Centre where excellent Bradford band, The Cresters, were enjoying a full house as result of the over-subscribed Beatles gig."

In November that year, The Beatles finally headlined Sheffield City Hall in their own right – they'd already performed there numerous times over in the past months as part of bigger package tours as support to the likes of Helen Shapiro and Roy Orbison.

Star newspaper journalist Francis Mullions described it as "the night when Sheffield went Beatle-barmy" and tells the story of thousands of "frenzied screamagers" yelling themselves hoarse.

The relative security of a limo.

Janis Riley: "I remember the day after The Beatles concert I went outside the Grand Hotel. All the pop groups used to stay there. John Lennon and Paul McCartney were on the veranda waving at us all, which was quite nice. Everybody knew they were staying there so there were a lot of people waiting to catch a glimpse of them.

"I saw The Beatles twice in Sheffield and the Rolling Stones once. I thought the sixties was a total revolution in music. I feel privileged to have been a part of that."

Above: The Beatles meeting fans at Sheffield City Hall.

There were faintings and hundreds of fans were still outside the stage door at midnight not realising the band had actually left within seconds of finishing – they didn't even bother changing out of their stage clothes, they just ran!

Joan Morris: "We'd been counting down the days to the show for weeks. We were absolutely Beatle-crazy. The screaming was bad enough before they started but when they appeared it was absolute pandemonium.

"I could hardly recognise a song all night – it was impossible over the noise of the hysterics. A girl near us fainted – I can remember it plain as day. Once she was okay she just started screaming again!"

There was no less chaos backstage either. The band – or at least their entourage – managed to snub Olympic long jumper Sheila Parkin who'd previously arranged to present them with a Top Stars Special Popularity Poll Award. When the Sheffield athlete turned up she was told the band were too tired to see anyone.

All came good after Brian Epstein invited her on an all expenses paid trip to London to meet the band. She also won silver at the 1968 Olympics and gold at the 1970 Commonwealth Games so it wasn't a bad era for her really.

The Beatles said thank you and good night to the city on Wednesday, December 8, 1965, when they performed at the Gaumont as part of the band's final British tour.

They totally outwitted the fans again. Whilst they were in hysterics laying siege to the stage door hours before the show, The Beatles simply pulled up outside the main public entrance and walked straight in!

Ringo said at the time: "It was unusual for us. Normally we had to hide in vans or go in through back entrances. They did not know what was going on."

The Top Stars Special snub was not repeated. Compere Jerry Stevens of Gleadless presented them with two awards whilst they were on stage.

The Beatles visited Sheffield several times as part of package tours supporting the like of Helen Shapiro and Roy Orbison, who is pictured on the brochure they're reading.

In 1963 Alan Burke's dad was PC 541 Ken Burke, a police driver.

Alan: "He was a driver at the time attached to the CID. He used to drive the vans that raided the illegal drinking dens that the Jamaican immigrants used to hold in the cellars of their houses down Attercliffe. When the Beatles came to Sheffield City Hall dad came home from his shift with the traffic division.

And that evening he had a very different job: "He told me that he smuggled the Beatles into the back of the City Hall dressed as policemen. They were loaded into the back of a Black Mariah (paddy wagon). My dad drove up to the artists' entrance, they opened the back door and rushed them in through the throng of fans – who never realised it was the Beatles!"

CHAPTER 5

READY STEADY **WENT**

Trafalgar Square with the National Gallery in the background. Linda's big adventure.

I t's testament to the longevity of one of the sixties most enduring pop shows that more than 50 years since it first hit the screens it's title is still a byword for modernist cool.

Ready Steady Go! (or *RSG* as it became better known) was first broadcast in August 1963. Despite running for only three years its legacy and influence show no sign of abating. Indeed it was a highlight of the 2011 Meltdown Festival when Kinks' frontman Ray Davies recreated it.

Linda Biggs looking the part.

Most local pop fans had to make do with watching it on the TV. But one Chesterfield resident, Linda Biggs (Hardy at the time), went one better and was lucky enough to travel to London to see the show being recorded.

She had a friend, Barbara, in Chesterfield whose dad worked on the railways and in the early sixties he was transferred back to his home territory of East London. Although Linda has since lost touch with Barbara she recalls that their Chesterfield home was on the site of what is now the Ibis Hotel.

Linda: "I had no idea that my impending trip to London to stay with my friend and her parents would result in me being lucky enough to visit my favourite TV pop show.

"I'll explain: It was after leaving school in June 1965, and before I started my junior clerk job in early July. My parents allowed me to travel alone to London to stay with Barbara and her parents in Manor Park, East London.

"I regarded it as a bit of an adventure. In fact everything about it was a huge thrill, from choosing what clothes and shoes to take, my hair rollers, lacquer and precious tail-comb, together with little gifts for my friend and her parents.

"My mum was paranoid that I'd lose my money so she made me stash ten bob notes into various pockets in my luggage, so it wasn't all kept in my purse. It was a great idea of hers and I still do it today!

"In those days, we didn't have a house phone, and neither did my friend, so everything had to be arranged by letter. Barbara's mum wrote to my mum to confirm everything with a promise to be at Victoria Coach Station to meet me.

"My mum waved me off and several hours later I was met with smiles and big hugs. Barbara's mum was a proper Cockney with a fabulous outlook on life and a hilarious way of pronouncing things. She knew we called everyone 'duck' up North and her version of that was to ask me 'You OK then, mah dack?' Or 'Ja wanna cappa tea, dack?'

"The freedom Barbara had was incredible. Although we couldn't leave her house without

"I regarded it as a bit of an adventure. In fact everything about it was a huge thrill, from choosing what clothes and shoes to take, my hair rollers, lacquer and precious tail-comb, together with little gifts for my friend and her parents.

having a pep talk from her mum about being extra careful in certain areas, and we were definitely not to talk to strangers or anyone who approached us in the street. After said talk we were good to go. We'd get the tube at East Ham and travel into the city, walking for miles, taking in all the sights.

"After a couple of days being shown the highlights of London, culture lost its appeal and Barbara decided I needed to see Soho! We scuttled through the naughty area and came out near Carnaby Street. I'd only ever read about Carnaby Street and was chuffed to bits to actually be there. I was totally in awe of the place and the fabulous shops we went in – Mary Quant!

"We couldn't afford anything but we stood in gazing at the beautiful designs and colours. The shop itself was much smaller than I imagined and the assistants were very sassy looking girls, if a little haughty. As two 15-year-olds with not much money we were not likely to buy anything in there, so as I recall, we were largely ignored.

"Out in the street, fascinating people walked past in fashions I'd only seen in magazines, and which had not yet made it to Chesterfield. Girls wearing pretty shirt type dresses, or 'A' line shifts in colour blocks, with many sporting berets or peaked caps. Op Art monochrome was one of the most striking features of sixties fashion and it festooned the shop windows everywhere.

"The boys were sartorially elegant in their beautifully cut suits from shops like Lord John. I wondered how on earth they could afford them, but of course they were older than me and had jobs. In my navy mini skirt and white short sleeved jumper, with flesh coloured tights and Hush

Puppies on my feet I felt positively dowdy, but that was pretty normal fashion where I came from.

"Later that day we found ourselves in a big department store on Oxford Street where things were more affordable. So despite not having a lot of money to spend on myself I decided my meagre wardrobe needed a bit of a perk up. I treated myself to some huge daisy earrings with bright yellow centres and long white petals.

"Barbara spotted some white tights with a lacy design, so we both bought some. Then I really pushed the boundaries and added some false eyelashes to complete the purchase. That was the best part of two quid gone so I was skint then. Poor Barbara had to buy us both lunch in a Wimpy.

"I was so excited at the prospect of RSG. I have a recollection of Barbara having some sort of pass for us both and being told my name was Janet if anyone asked. I have no idea where or how she got the passes, but I do recall she had friends in stage school who may have auditioned so it could have been via them. We queued outside for quite a long time and the girls seemed to outnumber the boys. They were all London kids with accents so different to mine.

"We were told to gather round and dance near the platform of the artist performing at the time, look happy and applaud. The cameras were all over the place and moved around the room, so if you were not paying attention you were likely to get run over or walloped at the side of the head by a rotating camera! I'm not sure I actually realised

Linda sports a psychedelic dress as she shows off her first car.

251 CNN

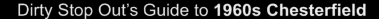
I was taking part in something quite so iconic, though I was in awe of the celebrities – especially Cathy McGowan; I was struck by her very shiny hair and her brightly coloured trouser suit.

"I remember seeing The Rolling Stones, The Yardbirds, and The Kinks. It was the summer of 1965.

"Some of the girls went out of their way to be noticed by dressing and dancing flamboyantly. I noticed lots of very long hair, back-combed hair, short skirts, modest skirts, bright colours in clothing. Boys in their suits with button down collared shirts. Boys with dodgy hair. The dance moves were very jerky at the time, with lots of balancing on one foot while waving the other one in front.

"We queued for what seemed like hours after the show so everyone was chatting while the time passed. Barbara and I were at the back of the crowd and we only knew someone notable had emerged when the screaming started. Being so much taller than her and with a lot of jumping up and down I could see it was Ray Davies. He

signed a few books then disappeared inside again. Barbara and I had no chance and we were hugely disappointed as both of us had a 'thing' for Ray Davies. We noticed that the seasoned autograph hunters were very pushy and ruthless and as a result we missed several opportunities, particularly The Rolling Stones.

"After a lull in anyone else famous coming out, some of the hunters began to drift away. This worked in our favour as we found ourselves in just a small but hopeful crowd. As a result, I was fortunate to get Jeff Beck's autograph.

"We caught the tube back to East London. We were a bit giggly because of our experience and I remember us getting told off by a man in the next seat because we were making too much noise. We just moved seats and continued to giggle.

"I think *Ready Steady Go!*'s importance in the 1960s was down to its young producers and directors absorption of the Mod culture. They steered away from rock and roll with the new genre of R'n'B and anything mod related. It

Linda saw The Rolling Stones, The Kinks and The Yardbirds at RSG and she got Jeff Beck's autograph (left in the Yardbirds shot).

Yardbirds

Kinks

Rolling Stones

also brought us soul music from America and eventually the wonderful motown. In my view it couldn't fail.

"The music scene had already begun to change with the arrival of rock 'n' roll in the late fifties, showcased by programmes like *Six Five Special, Oh Boy!* and *Boy Meets Girl*. Such programmes were favoured by my parents' generation and I remember vividly my dad's younger sister teaching me to jive to Chuck Berry and Jerry Lee Lewis when I was about eight years old. That was in her back kitchen with the rug rolled up and thrown outside!

"I loved Friday's because of RSG, particularly so after I'd been to the show. I'd hurry my tea and get settled in front of the telly in anticipation. My mum wasn't too fussed and even moaned about Dusty Springfield: 'Too much eye make up. I don't know how she can see out of her eyes!'

"It was a sad day when RSG reached its end. In fact I mourned its loss, absolutely convinced it couldn't be bettered. But of course by that time Top Of The Pops had launched and I often wonder if TOTP was RSG's death-knell. I preferred RSG for the music even though some of the camera shots messed with my eyes – so much quick zooming! Then as with most things, you gradually move on and RSG became a distant memory. Distant it may be, hazy to a certain extent but definitely not forgotten."

Many say the show's passing left a gaping hole in the cultural fabric of the UK that has never truly been filled. There's little doubt it set the benchmark for everything that followed.

Indeed speaking in 2011 Ray Davies said: "There's something missing from our culture now, that kind of show. Yes, we have *The X Factor*, but *Ready Steady Go!* allowed the performers to be themselves, they weren't manufactured."

Ready Steady Go! totally rewrote the script in terms of youth orientated programming and became a Friday night must-see for the younger generation.

Its minimalist style employed little in the way of scenery, costumes, choreography or make-up. It was totally at odds with the established world of light entertainment.

Though the musicians were the stars, the audience were almost on a par as they milled around the various stages, danced and got in the way of the cameras as they battled their way to film the next act. The show went out at 6pm on a Friday evening.

The immortal line, "The weekend starts here!" rang out to herald its arrival before the opening notes of *Wipe Out* by Surfaris (the intro tune was later replaced by Manfred Mann's *5-4-3-2-1*, then Manfred Mann's *Hubble Bubble, Toil and Trouble*, then, finally, the Rolling Stones with *Goin' Home*).

Ready Steady Go! provided a far more informal offering than Top Of The Pops which appeared a year later on the BBC.

The audience was hand-picked from hip London clubs – later joined by other members provided by venues in the provinces – to ensure they were always in tune with the artists. They would surround the musicians as they performed on mini-stages, studio gantries or on the studio floor itself.

The show made an overnight star of presenter Cathy McGowan who was soon overshadowing the programme's original frontman, Keith Fordyce. Being of a similar age to much of the show's audience and an ardent fan of the acts she went on to introduce and interview, her inexperience and easy going style gelled with musicians and viewers alike.

McGowan's adoption of the latest trendy shift

Ready Steady Go! totally rewrote the script in terms of youth orientated programming and became a Friday night must-see for the younger generation.

and mini-dresses made her a fashion icon and her use of teenage slang – things either got the thumbs up for being 'fab' or 'smashing' or thumbs down for being 'square' or 'out' – encapsulated the rebellious nature of the programme.

The Mary Quant-looking presenter was dubbed 'Queen of the mods' with *Ready Steady Go!* soon adopted by the fast growing modernist movement that boasted acts spanning The Who to the Small Faces as their standard bearers.

One observer compared the programme to "a King's Road party where the performers themselves had only just chanced to drop by". It was 50 percent style and 50 percent chaos.

George Shaw said: *"Ready Steady Go!* was an absolute must for anyone even vaguely interested in youth orientated music and fashion – I never missed a single edition despite my parents banning me from watching it altogether at one point. They hated it. I ended up going to my friends house to watch it where attitudes were rather more relaxed!"

The show would never have been allowed to happen at the prudish BBC at that point. By the end of the second year of the show it had broken dozens of acts in the UK.

So many artists that went on to be household names made their TV debut on *Ready, Steady, Go!*

They included The Beatles, the Rolling Stones, the Kinks, the Animals, the Who, Manfred Mann, Sandie Shaw, the Walker Brothers, Lulu, Dusty Springfield, the Searchers, the Pretty Things, the Yardbirds and Jimi Hendrix.

Dusty Springfield persuaded Vicki Wickham, one of the show's producers, to do a Motown special that she fronted. It included Stevie Wonder, the Miracles and Martha and the Vandellas. That night helped launch soul music in the UK.

The Supremes performed their *Stop! In the Name of Love* dance routine for the first time the same night.

There was also a Who special appropriately titled, *Ready Steady Who!*

The BBC eventually realised it needed to come up with something to compete. Its answer was *Top of the Pops*. It lacked the style and edgy improvised chaos of *Ready Steady Go!* but it

did have one advantage; the top 20 chart was published on Thursdays and the BBC was given the lowdown two days earlier.

The producers cast and scripted the show on Tuesdays, then rehearsed and broadcast it on Wednesday. To know who was new in the chart, or which song had gone to No 1, you had to watch it. Gradually they started pulling in the larger audience.

RSG producer Vicki Wickham said: "We were all so naive. It was like being given a box of candies and being able to eat them all. Elkan Allan, the executive producer, just said to us, book who you want. So we were booking people our own age, and for all sorts of reasons – Brian Jones, because we loved his hair and thought he was gorgeous. George Best, who we all thought was heavenly – he came on to be interviewed. We could have anyone."

Peter Stringfellow: *"In 1966 I was a warm-up with* Ready Steady Go! *That started as I was in London trying to sell the first record by the band I was managing at the time, Johnny Tempest and the Cadillacs. I came down to try and get them on the show and I met up with the editor, Vickie Wickham.*

"She was impressed with the way I came over. They must have been looking for a new 'boy' presenter for the programme to help Cathy McGowan. Out of the blue she said 'your group's very good but we'd like you to come and try out for the programme'.

"I couldn't get my breath! So I went down and did what I thought was my version of what was required. I had no idea what my style was. I just did what I did and this was definitely before my ad-libbing was honed down. In those days anything came out of my mouth!

"They decided they liked me but they weren't going to use me straight away. I ended up becoming 'the warm up man' for Ready Steady Go! *That meant I warmed up the audience and did things with them for the camera.*

"They'd say we need people dancing over there and I'd get a bunch of people dancing – always making sure I was involved! So every time they were on camera, I was on camera!

"As I started on Ready Steady Go! *and booking bands in Sheffield for my King Mojo I started going to the Flamingo in London. It was the place you went to see the new R'n'B bands. I was booking bands from the Flamingo like Georgie Fame and Graham Bond Organisation.*

"This was my first introduction to late night London. We'd say, what time's Georgie Fame on and they'd say one o'clock. And we'd say what time?! And they'd say 'one o'clock in the morning'.

"I bet we came to see him three times and each

Peter Stringfellow was a warm-up with **Ready Steady Go! In 1966.**

time we fell asleep beforehand! The London guys were much hipper than us. The Flamingo was a musicians' hangout – there was a lot of black musicians.

"In fact there was a split – you didn't play the Marquee at that time if you were black. You played the Flamingo if you were black or white.

"We'd come down in cars with no heaters and get as far as Finchley and get really excited. To us, London girls looked yellow. Sheffield girls would wear make-up at night but never in the day. In London they wore it in the day.

"You'd never fill the car up with petrol in those days. You'd put in two gallons and see how far you got. You'd then stop and maybe put another gallon in if you could afford it.

"London was where the real names were coming through. The Yardbirds wouldn't play the Flamingo – they'd play the Marquee and Eel Pie Island. To get to Eel Pie Island you'd need to head out of central London to Putney. We'd be going to Bag O' Nails or Scotch of St James after Ready Steady Go!"

CHAPTER 6

ONE GIANT LEAP FOR MANKIND

O n Sunday, July 20 1969 the Apollo 11 space flight landed the first two humans on the Moon. Six hours later mission commander Neil Armstrong who had made the lunar touch-down with pilot Buzz Aldrin, would become the first person to set foot on the lunar surface. Aldrin soon joined him.

On the same day in another corner of the solar system – namely a field in Bolsover, north Derbyshire – two intrepid teenagers, Tom Bailey and Paul Hobday, were taking their first tentative steps on the voyage of discovery that would make them life-long musical performers.

While history was being made on the moon, back on planet Earth the bright petals of flower power were still glistening in the eternal sunshine of the endless Summer of Love, and many young troubadours were marshalling their talents to spread peace and good vibes across the land through music and song.

While history was being made on the moon, back on planet Earth the bright petals of flower power were still glistening in the eternal sunshine of the endless Summer of Love

Chesterfield was no stranger to the aspirant minstrel and Tom and Paul were two of the keenest. So it came to pass that Witching Hour was born – a four-piece psychedelic electric folk band featuring frontman Des Parry on vocals and guitar, backed by Paul on guitar, Tom on bass and John Walker on the drums (he would later play for metal-ish outfit Son of a Bitch – SOB – which later morphed into Saxon, sadly not with him behind the kit).

The most significant name in the list is that of Tom Bailey who went on to form the Thompson Twins in the late 1970s (with your author amongst others) and took the band to global stardom in the 1980s.

Witching Hour performed only a couple of times in their short career, but their debut certainly made an impression – as a support act

Your two correspondents Paul Hobday and Tom Bailey (left and centre) with your author Pete Dodd captured in the glare of a spotlight outside Chesterfield Town Hall in the same year as the Bolsover gig. None of us remember this photo being taken and had never seen it until 2018. Photographer John Ashforth recalls we were trying to replicate the cover of the Goodbye Cream album. It would appear at least two of us had no idea what it looked like. Tom bought his cords from Mr Six. The colour? Wheat. I am wearing my mum's war time duffel coat (Colour: camel). She was a Wren (Women's Royal Naval Service – WRNS) in the women's branch of the Royal Navy. Having learned French and German at St Helena's school she was employed by our armed forces intercepting enemy messages on the south coast of England – and that coat, big enough to fit over her regular Navy togs, came in useful on those chill winter nights.

to anarchist Mick Farren's Deviants at an open air concert in Bolsover, with security provided by the local chapter of the Hell's Angels.

That sunny afternoon concert marked Tom's first public performance on the bass guitar, the same instrument he would later choose to start blazing the Thompson trail as a professional musician.

Tom dredges his mid-teen memory banks: "My recollection of this is patchy, but I do recall Pete Dodd introducing me to Paul Hobday as someone who had recently joined a band with local semi-legend Des Parry who thrashed a red Hofner Verithin.

"Pete and I were impressed enough to want to attend a rehearsal at drummer John Walker's attic in the home of his parents which was down a rather sinister looking dead-end alley off Beetwell Street long since demolished (now home to the town's cop shop).

"At some point in the rehearsal of Des' soft psychedelica I must have picked up a tambourine and joined in. Next thing, at his insistence, I was miked up."

"It was relatively close to the Salvation Army building and that was to cause us problems later when they complained of the disruptive noise during their Sunday services.

"Paul was late because the coffin look-alike guitar case which he had made in school woodwork class proved too heavy to carry on its first outing. We traipsed up to the attic through a miasma of unpleasant feline odours, meeting John's parents on the way.

"His brother was also present and, at some point, he grabbed the mic and sang an Elvis standard (*Blue Suede Shoes*, perhaps). Symbolically, he seemed part of the old 'teddy boy' rockers culture whereas, in my mind at least, we were part of the new vanguard of the free-thinking and stylistically liberated hippy movement (Dream on, Ed.) – a social group referred to locally and pejoratively as 'magics' by local wits and skinheads. Des Parry's long hair seemed evidence enough that we were part of that group.

"At some point in the rehearsal

Deviants frontman Mick Farren.

John Walker played the drums for Witching Hour at the Bolsover gig.

of Des' soft psychedelica I must have picked up a tambourine and joined in. Next thing, at his insistence, I was miked up – and shortly after that invited to join the band. We were named Witching Hour on that day. There was an old bass guitar lying around and no player, so I became the bassist even though I'd never touched one before.

"There was much talk of the fact that we had been booked to open for counterculture legends The Social Deviants (abbreviated to The Deviants before the gig), a vehicle for the writing and musical performance of Mick Farren who was already a notorious serial commentator in such essential alternative rags as the International Times (IT) and OZ.

"At least, that's what I was subsequently told by local long-haired Marc Bolan obsessive Richard Taylor who was buzzing about Farren's connection with Steve Peregrine Took from T(yrannosaurus)-Rex and his friend Twink. These were the names of unapproachable gods to our small-town mentality, so the idea that they were coming to a local festival and that we were to play before them seemed to put an extra froth on everybody's pint of mild at the Queen's Head.

"By this time, due to a policy of passive permissiveness, the pub was rapidly becoming the hangout of underage drinkers with flared trousers and maxi skirts. Coincidentally, another popular watering hole of the period was close to John's place – the Queen's Park Hotel. It was the venue for Chesterfield Folk Club meetings and the weapon of choice was a bottled beer called 'Luncheon'. I think it was 12p a pint and the place was probably knocked down by the same bulldozers which levelled John's family home.

"Anticipation was soon peaking for the Bolsover event. Paul announced that his brother Dennis

had agreed to drive us there in his vintage car ("with running boards") and this was deemed to be the sort of style statement coup which would announce our presence to the world.

"We had absurdly misplaced notions of our own brilliance and chances of success. In the event, as the old banger trundled onto the Bolsover grass, nobody noticed. What they possibly did see, much to my teenage embarrassment, was the result of my having submitted to the indignity of a haircut (dramatically close to a short back and sides) on the previous day. Nevertheless, we were decked out in flared cords, paisley shirts and, I seem to remember, some beads. Des Parry sported burgundy crushed velvet loons, so we were probably safe.

"The gig itself was a blur. We were accommodated cheerfully by the Deviants' stage crew. I was plugged into their bass backline and was immediately unable to control the feedback or hear the other instruments. I was utterly out of

"I was too busy adrift on a tidal wave of adrenaline and enjoying the vague feeling that I was a 'part of something'. Dazed by the experience – and having promised to come home early to do my homework."

The Deviants circa 1969.

my depth and the performance must have been appallingly bad, but I couldn't tell.

"I was too busy adrift on a tidal wave of adrenaline and enjoying the vague feeling that I was a 'part of something'. Dazed by the experience – and having promised to come home early to do my homework – I don't remember much about the Deviants set other than it being hard rock/early metal in style.

"Tall, skinny and afro-topped Farren's performance was energetic and confrontational. It included references to "screwing" which seemed enough to confirm the event's credentials as a part of something much bigger: the socio-sexual revolution which was believed to be in the air at that time, even in Chesterfield.

"Although I admit to the laughable naivety of all this, I now honestly miss the era when undercurrents in rock'n'roll and even more blatantly mainstream popular music seemed to carry along rebellious promises of social change in a way which the establishment could not control. That was exciting for so many reasons beyond the mere sounds and songs of the time. I know that some of those promises were not kept, but others have endured and opened our lives to change.

"On a personal note, this was my first gig on bass. The fact is, I went on to become a professional bassist in later years, but as can be seen from this story, the choice of instrument was thrust upon me by happenstance. Ain't that the way things happen?"

Though Witching Hour was short-lived, like Tom, Paul Hobday, continued to play music all his life. He tours internationally, accompanying his long-term musical collaborator, the singer, songwriter, guitarist Steve Payne and is at the vanguard of the lively music scene in Chepstow, Monmouthshire.

Paul's and Tom's independent accounts, dear reader, chime remarkably well 50 years later giving a lie to the notion that if you can remember the sixties you weren't really there. One of the many things in common was vigorous parental interference in both their attempts to achieve the tripped out sartorial elegance of the day.

Paul: "Pete Dodd lived across the road from me, and we spent hours sitting around his record player listening to Small Faces 45s and Syd Barrett's Pink Floyd album *The Piper At The Gates Of Dawn*.

"We learned to play the songs on cheap second-hand guitars. I looked to Pete for which records to pay attention to (still do!), and Pete generally left it to me to work out guitar parts. Soon we were

One of the support bands listed for the concert was King Mob Echo whose bass player at the time was Mick Twelves. But it comes as news to him.
Mick: "I have not the faintest recollection of this gig – but I do remember staying in a squat in Holland Park and borrowing Mick Farren's motorbike to ride over to Notting Hill Gate."

joined by John Roog (another founding Thompson Twin) and Tom, and we would 'jam' for hours – learning from each other along the way.

"Pete and I happened upon a band rehearsing, called Hell Let Loose, led by a long haired hipster called Des Parry. I immediately was riveted by Des's speedy, wild playing and persuaded him to teach me. He invited me to his parent's house and I was deeply impressed by his psychedelic bedroom decorated in random pastel colours and with a Union Jack painted on the ceiling. He taught me *Hey Joe* by Jimi Hendrix and I was hooked.

"On the ground floor, John's mum couldn't hear a thing while we thrashed away on the top floor. We made what must have been an appalling racket."

"Before long, a band was formed with me and Des on guitars, Tom on bass, and John Walker on drums. We rehearsed at John's house, which was a four storey ramshackle property opposite a funeral directors, down a dingy blind lane which could have been an inspiration for Harry Potter's Diagon Alley.

"On the ground floor, John's mum couldn't hear a thing while we thrashed away on the top floor. We made what must have been an appalling racket. Certainly, that was the opinion of a TV crew who were filming the cricket at Queen's Park! They demanded that we stop. We opened the windows wide. Well, why not? We would be heard on TV!

"To my memory we only played two gigs. The second was at a club – it was called Necromancer I think. But our first gig was a real coup – an open air concert, no less.

"My mother, having been a professional actress, had certain 'standards' when it came to presenting oneself on stage, and so when she saw me, ready to go and play my first 'big' gig dressed in bleached Levis, grandad shirt and sandals she hit the roof.

"The ensuing argument is embossed upon my memory to this day. She literally barred the way to the front door, and made me go and change into cavalry twill 'slacks' and a sports jacket. The crippling embarrassment!

"I ditched the jacket, and borrowed some jeans – and one of Des Parry's numerous chiffon scarves, but I swore that day that if I ever had kids, I would never do anything similar to them. Arriving in style in my brother's Morris 10 (we called it his Elliot Ness wagon) I unloaded my equipment.

"I look back with disbelief. I jest not – I had an eight watt hi-fi amplifier, which sat proudly on top of a Mateus Rose crate with an eight-inch Wharfedale hi-fi speaker in it!

"The Deviants had a backline of six-foot high Simms Watts 100 watt stacks and could easily have been forgiven for laughing at us as a bunch of rank amateurs (Which you were, Ed.). But no, they very kindly gave us the use of the Deviants' backline.

"Tom and I instantly discovered that if you stand right next to a 100 watt stack and plug in with the guitar volume full up, the uncontrollable feedback is something to behold! The road crew intervened and soon we were ready to play. I can't remember much about the gig – we must have been bloody awful, that's for certain, but it was the embryo from which all of us developed musically and continue to do so.

"About ten years ago, I found Des Parry on a social media site. I telephoned him, and despite me describing his bedroom in Chesterfield, the Bolsover gig, and learning *Hey Joe* – he had absolutely no recollection of me, Tom, John, or any of the above – and even less interest in keeping in touch!"

SUNDAY, JULY 20

BOLSOVER: Pop concert the open air at Sherwood Lodge, Bolsover, with the Deviants, King Mob Echo & Hanover Sauare. Adm 5/-. 2.30pm.

From Bolsover to Brian Eno

Headliners, The Deviants, may have been part of the thumping heart of the counter culture but that didn't add up to any big deal in the environs of Chesterfield. Their brand of rough-round-the-edges garage/acid rock was an acquired taste to bucolic country folk and the open air shindig was hardly bustling. Early on in proceedings frontman Mick Farren, in rich cockney tones probably never heard before in the shadow of Bolsover Castle, unsuccessfully urged the punters to: "Stop sittin' round in little clumps." Or 'clamps' as it issued from the Farren larynx.

Nevertheless, those who did fork out the required five shillings to attend the event were witnessing the start of something significant that would inform the coming hipster years.

According to the Guardian's Farren obituary from 2013, publisher Felix Dennis, described him as: "a doorman, editor, journalist, rock star, rabble rouser, critic and commentator, charlatan, jester, impresario, gunslinging cross-dresser, icon, author, songwriter, poet". Ahead of his time, perhaps.

His musical exploits were matched by his adventures in writing. After a spell as editor of the aforementioned IT, he joined and transformed the *New Musical Express (NME)*, along with several other 'alternative' scribes of the time including Charles Shaar Murray (whose reputation was already established as a contributor to Schoolkids' OZ) and Nick Kent.

Farren always kept his musical ambitions alive and it was perhaps fitting he died in July 2013, aged 69, having collapsed on stage while performing with a new Deviants line-up at the Borderline Club in London, during the Atomic Sunshine one-day festival.

Deviants guitarist Paul Rudolph went on to play with Brian Eno.

The guitarist on that Bolsover day was Canadian Paul Rudolph who would soon afterwards form the Pink Fairies with former Pretty Things drummer Twink. He would also develop associations with the Hawkwind massive, which resulted in a meeting with Brian Eno.

As a result, Eno employed Rudolph's guitar services on much of his post-Roxy Music 1970s solo work including *Here Come the Warm Jets* (where Rudolph plays a blistering solo often attributed to Robert Fripp on the track *Baby's On Fire*), *Another Green World* and *Before and After Science*.

He later returned to Canada to concentrate on a very different discipline – professional cycling.

Below: Sarsaparilla or a (usually frozen) Jubbly? Drinks of distinction for young sixties Chesterfield Stop Outs.

Paul Hobday was only ever passing through Chesterfield – the result of his father securing a retail job for a while in Clay Cross – and he left still a teenager. But during his stay, the town left indelible images tattooed for ever on the back of his mind:
"Battered slices of potato from the chippy on Chester Street (Potato scallops, I do believe – Ed.).
"Walking through Robinson's factory site on the way to William Rhodes School and feeling intimidated by gangs of factory girls.
"Sarsaparilla from Shabby Wayne's, the little shop on Old Road.
"The Hulley's bus to Baslow.
"Hanging out in the coolest shop in town – Some Kinda Mushroom – and coveting that electric blue Telecaster in Hudson's music shop.
"Having a schoolboy crush on a waitress twice my age in the coffee shop on Glumangate (The Studio, now Pinnochio's – Ed.).

"Rolling Old Holborn cigs in the Wimpy bar.
"Becoming aware of local 'faces' like Mick Twelves – effortlessly cool.
"The Millership brothers – scary Harley Davidson riding rebels (and official 'security' at the Bolsover gig).
"And 'Gessler' (the formidable skinhead and football rowdy named after William Tell's arch enemy) who allegedly pierced a guy's ear with a dart plucked from a pub dartboard.
"These are my random memories of Chesterfield in the late sixties – but the defining theme for me was music – and it is with me still."

Arguably the only 'true' mod band, the Small Faces charted a natural course from 'modness' to magic madness. Even their songs blatantly referenced the recreational drugs of the day. Here Come The Nice was about the mods' drug of choice with the tell-tale lyric referring to their drug dealer: "He knows what I want/He's got what I need/ He's always there/If I need some speed". They followed through with blatant acid anthems My Mind's Eye and the evergreen Itchycoo Park.

Magics

Young Brampton mod Jenny Crowley is seen here enjoying all the fun of the fair with her friend Alison. She is also pictured in Llandudno with a long forgotten mod surfer and elsewhere on the sea front.

CHAPTER 7

OF MODS AND MAGICS

Pete Coleman was a pupil at Chesterfield School (Clarke House) in the mid to late sixties. He studied to be a 'Stop Out' via the 'mod' and 'magic' disciplines.

Pete: "I must have been about 15 when I first visited the Vic and I think it was with an older friend called Tim Robinson. I remember walking into Jonny Johnson and the Bandwagon. *Breaking Down The Walls of Heartache* which blew me away: a large ballroom, loads of people – including girls! – all washed down with a diamond and lime.

"That was Saturday night sorted for next year or so until it was closed down. All the live bands downstairs in 'The (Velvet) Underground', then upstairs to the disco.

The last night of the Vic featured the band Yes. The place got ripped to pieces. I wonder if some people still have their souvenirs?

Pete recalls that when the band Free played there was the usual advert in the *Derbyshire Times* for the Saturday night with the word 'Free' under an advert for the Vic, leading to some disappointment among the punters on arrival at the box office.

Pete recalls the routine: "I used to come to Taaan most nights by the time I was 16. I met John Bradshaw who was on the 6.40 from Holymoorside and went to White's Bar (how did we afford it?). Mondays we went on to the Vic and later after it closed down, the Odeon Ballroom.

"Wednesdays I seem to think we went to the Adam and Eve or the Purple Haze next to the bowl. Friday and Saturday it was the Vic and Sunday the Carlton Club on Whittington Moor. You got chicken in a basket and I think a drink for the entrance fee (2/6d rings a bell).

"Sometimes I teamed up with Al Tagg and the scooter boys. I was his co-pilot for a while and then I bought a bike of my own. Never really did the Skeggy thing, thankfully, but had a few skirmishes in Sheffield going to the Top Rank. And the 'Riot in Ripley' was a memorable night.

"The aforementioned Al Tagg went to the same school (Large house) and was in the year above Pete.

Al has his own recollections of the period: "In 1968 I was a 15-year-old mod growing up in Chesterfield. The 'scene' was made up of a few places. Whites Bar, now part of the Golden Fleece, was, as I recall, somewhere we went on a Saturday lunchtime – drinking Double Diamond under age. The Burlington Grill was another place to |hang out on a Saturday afternoon, one cup of coffee for as long as you could get away with it.

Pete Coleman sidesteps the scooter and goes straight for a 'chopper'. Very Easy Rider.

"The Vic was two nights a week, one week night and then Saturday night. I liked to hang out in the upstairs balcony bar, which gave a good view of the dance floor below. David McPhie was the resident DJ. I remember one night he was so fed up of playing Wooly Bully he said anybody could come up and smash his vinyl 45. So I did – a good laugh."

McPhie has clarified since that it was the endless repetition of the song, rather than the song itself, that provoked the record breaking offer that Al Tagg took up. The 1965 dance-floor smash Wooly Bully *by Sam the Sham and the Pharaohs was originally called* Hully Gully *after the dance of the same name but was changed because a song with that title already existed. The reference in the lyric to "not be L-7" is, of course to "not be square":*

Uno, dos, one, two, tres, quatro
Matty told Hatty about a thing she saw
Had two big horns and a wooly jaw.
Wooly bully, wooly bully
Wooly bully, wooly bully, wooly bully
Hatty told Matty, let's don't take no chance
Let's not be L-7, come and learn to dance
Wooly bully, wooly bully
Wooly bully, wooly bully, wooly bully
Matty told Hatty, that's the thing to do
Get you someone really to pull the wool
with you
Wooly bully, wooly bully
Wooly bully, wooly bully, wooly bully

Sara Oldfield

Internationally eminent botanist Sara Oldfield was appointed Officer of the Order of the British Empire (OBE) in the 2016 Birthday Honours for services to the conservation and protection of wild tree species worldwide.

An accomplished author with scores of books and research papers to her name, she was Secretary General of Botanic Gardens Conservation International (BGCI) for ten years from May 2005. Previously she worked as Global Programmes Director for Fauna and Flora International.

Sara has worked for a wide range of other conservation organisations, including UNEP World Conservation Monitoring Centre and Royal Botanic Gardens, Kew and also as a freelance consultant, working as a researcher and policy advisor for international biodiversity conservation.

But before all that, she danced round her handbag at the Vic! And she kept a teenage diary of her exploits. Here she leafs through its pages to remind herself of those halcyon days of yore:

"The first time I went to the Vic was on Saturday 28 December, 1968 aged 13 and three quarters. I thought it was 'great' but did not like the group, the Idle Race. Lily the Pink was number one in the charts.

"Over the next year cryptic entries in my diary record exam results at St Helena High School, the names of boys – mods and skinheads – I had seen in town (but I was too timid to speak to any male except my dad), and what I wore to the Vic, Odeon and Purple Haze.

"I also recorded, each week, which single was number one in the charts. On my 14th birthday, March 1, I went to the Vic and my friend Sian Lewis requested I'll Pick a Rose for My Rose by Marv Johnson for me. She also bought me half a pint of cider. Where Do You Go To My Lovely? by Peter Sarstedt was number one.

"On March 23, 1969 I went on 30-mile Shelter sponsored walk. Get Ready by the Temptations was number one.

"My musical tastes have scarcely progressed since 1969, although all time favourite Until You Come Back To Me by Aretha Franklin was a little later.

"Favourite memories of the Vic: definitely classic dancing round handbags to Tamla Motown. I also seem to remember watching the Upsetters at the Vic, but no mention in the diary. Perhaps the same night as the Idle Race."

Pete Coleman continues his reminiscences: "Another Saturday night regular was a trip to the Old English at Matlock. It might have been after the Vic closed down but it was around scooter time. We would catch a bus there from town after a pint or two. There was usually a bus full which was not a quiet affair as you can imagine.

"I remember we usually had a couple first because we were often dying for a leak by the time we got there. There was Derek Murray, myself, Al Tagg, John Bradshaw, Graham Storer and the usual hard cases like Dec Roberts, Micko, Spenner, and memorably John Merry (although not a hard case as such).

"He ended up in borstal or similar for glassing someone in the downstairs disco. He always maintained it was self defence. But it wasn't pretty. We were often escorted home by the local panda cars on the last bus sometime after 11.00. I think that was because people upstairs had a habit of throwing the seats out of the window.

"John and I got off at Walton Back Lane or the Blue Stoops and walked home which nicely avoided any fracas in town. Saturday nights usually ended at Wooton's fish and chip shop at Walton crossroads after a walk home from town. There were no late buses and amazingly by today's standards the chip shops stayed open really late."

The Big City

Pete also remembers forays to the Top Rank in Sheffield: "I remember taking a girl out who worked in Boots at the beauty counter as I had some tickets for the Fantastics (who had couple of Motown-style hits).

"The problem was the last train was at 11.30pm and the band didn't come on stage until 11pm. We saw the first number then had to run for the train. I don't think she was impressed and she dumped me.

"If a group went over then there were often scuffles and last minute chases to the train. One chap (can't remember his name) got picked up by the police for having a leak down the 'Hole in the Road' in the town

centre (Once upon a time a pedestrian underpass with shops at the centre of one of the city's road roundabouts.)

"We had previously cleared the Stonehouse as someone threw a glass across the room and everyone got split up as the police were out looking for us. It was said someone was arrested for trying to steal a milk float to get home, but these were all stories that were difficult to verify – though highly believable.

"There was a weekend trip to Scarborough with John Bradshaw, Clive Milward, a guy called Dump and Richard ('Snip') Hewitt and others. We were visiting Eddie Plater (a one time skinhead 'face' in Chesterfield because he moved there after his dad sold the Corner House at the top corner of Glumangate, and taken a pub there).

"That ended with most of the Chesterfield crowd spending the night in the nick as Dump had managed to annoy someone in the Penthouse disco. It got a bit nasty. I was wrapped around a local girl and managed to avoid the fracas.

"We slept in the back of a minivan, I think it was Snip's. Not with the girl I hasten to add as she insisted I walked her home half way round Scarborough and then said cheerio."

The Bowling Alley

Stamford Hill in the London borough of Hackney was the location of the first bowling alley in the UK, which opened in 1960. It was the start a new craze imported from the US, as bowling alleys started to spring up all over the country.

A Magnet Bowl arrived in Lordsmill Street in the late 1960s where the Siam Corner Thai Village restaurant is now and where the Adam and Eve nightclub once was.

Pete Coleman was actually in a bowling team – The Crusaders. He recalls that the team once came second to the Arabian Knights who boasted a local champion called Barry.

Pete: "Tim Robinson was with me in the team and a couple of others I can't remember. That was every Sunday morning for a while. I seem to think we had proper bowling shirts with The Crusaders written on. Should have kept mine."

These pics may well jog memories of Chesterfield's Magnet Bowl back in the sixties, even if they are images of another bowling alley in the Magnet chain.

Al Tagg had a similar experience: "Chesterfield bowling alley had recently opened and I was in a Saturday bowling league in a team called The Matchstick Men, named after *Pictures of Matchstick Men* by Status Quo. There was also a disco there, round the back in the basement. I think it was called Purple Haze.

"I had been in there one night and then came out and went round to the bowling alley entrance trying to talk my way in without paying.

"All of a sudden some guys came from inside and grabbed me, frog marched me into the managers office and gave me a good beating, breaking my nose. Apparently shortly after I had left the disco somebody had dropped a stink bomb and I had been seen leaving and was accused of it."

Pete Coleman recalls spending a fortune on a new Levi jacket which he wore to the bowling alley on its first outing: "Some girls who I was trying to impress proceeded to set about it with sandpaper from matchboxes to 'fade' it along the seams. It fell to bits."

Dream Team

If ever there was a bunch of Stop Outs-in-waiting it's this under 15s Chesterfield School football team from the 1967-68 season.

The fashionably bespectacled young man with the early hint of a mod haircut is none other than Al Tagg whose modernist adventures are chronicled here in these pages.

Sitting to his left is future star of the sporting firmament Geoff Miller. Now an OBE, Geoff played in 34 Tests and 25 One Day Internationals for England from 1976 to 1984. He played for Derbyshire from 1973 to 1986, captaining the side from 1979 to 1981, and returned in 1990 after playing for Essex between 1987 and 1989. He was an England selector from 2008 to 2013 and was appointed President of Derbyshire CCC in March 2014.

If any proof were needed that Chesterfield is the home of the gentleman, cricketer and journalist Simon Hughes referred to Miller in 1990 as being "the only remaining player who unfailingly visited the opposing team's dressing room after play to thank them for the game... and the last man to field at slip with a whoopee cushion up his jumper".

Miller also owned Moss & Miller, a sporting goods outlet in Brampton, with Chesterfield FC footballer Ernie Moss, for a number of years and became a popular after-dinner speaker.

He was appointed Officer of the Order of the British Empire (OBE) in the 2014 New Year Honours for services to cricket, following his retirement as an England selector.

Stuart Woolgar, bottom row third from the left, became a professional footballer playing for West Bromwich Albion and Doncaster Rovers. According to school team mate Trev Hubbard (bottom right), in his debut for West Brom Woolgar was up against Manchester United at Old Trafford facing the formidable trio of Bobby Charlton, George Best and Dennis Law.

No other player pictured in that Chesterfield School team rose to similar heights, though some say Norman Dolling claimed his 15 minutes of fame as a contestant on Jim Bowen's ITV darts-based game show *Bull's Eye*. But most of them would blossom into lads about Chesterfield town in the ensuing years.

Many have wondered where Ron Mihaly was on the day the picture was taken. Currently a Derbyshire County Councillor serving the communities of Boythorpe, Whitecotes and Brampton (Holmebrook), Ron was a prestigious sporting all rounder and rarely missed a photo opportunity.

Best Law Charlton

CS Football Team

Here's the team list in full:
Top row (l-r): John Harvey, Chris Powell, Mick Portas, Chris Pates, Al Tagg, Geoff Miller, Mr Fomison (teacher).
Bottom row (l-r): Norman Dolling, Brian Hawkins, Stewart Woolgar, Martin Pates, Tim Presswood, Kevin Alford. Trev Hubbard.

Swimming trophies

According to Pete, one of the people you had to know was Clive Millward: "I'm not sure why, but he was a year older and very good at football – and with girls – so that was probably why.

"When Chesterfield School won the NE Derbyshire swimming competition at the Manor School baths, I ended up with the individual freestyle shield and the overall team shield (cos we whupped them all!). Derek Murray was swimming for Tapton and was still on the side when I came in after my second length of the relay. Tapton came second as well. We were good!

"Anyway the point was that Clive was there or I bumped into him on the way home to the bus and he ended up helping me with a shield. A police car saw us, stopped and pulled us in for a grilling as to how we came by the shields. Basically they saw Clive, who had previous, and put two and two together.

"Whilst driving around I was shocked at how many of the lads about town the cops knew by name: 'Ooh look there's Dec over there, what's he up to, etc etc?' It was probably an exercise in putting the frighteners on and it worked. Suffice it to say they believed I had won them as I had a wet towel and trunks.

"I was supposed to go up in assembly and receive the trophies as I was captain but I bottled it and had the day off much to my shame."

Dedicated followers of fashion

Al Tagg: "We weren't the sharp suits type of mods but more denim jackets, Levi jeans and parkas. Levis were advertised as 'shrink to fit' so I ended up sitting in a bath of cold water wearing my new Levis. They never did 'shrink to fit' but I ended up dyed blue from the waist down for three weeks!

Pete Coleman started adopting the garb of the day when reggae/ska was the music of choice – Desmond Dekker, Elizabethan Reggae, the Upsetters etc.

Pete: "I didn't go as far as adopting the pork pie hat but skinhead clobber included the inevitable Doc Martins, Levi jacket and jeans if you could afford it or you nicked it from Douglas Turners' shop on the corner of the Market Hall.

"The smart choice was a Crombie coat with hanky and a stud in the top pocket, Sta-prest (sic) trousers, and shirts by Ben Sherman, Arnold Palmer or Fred Perry.

"The Burlington was the café of choice as you could sit in the window and totty spot. And diagonally across next to the Williams and Glyns Bank was a clothes shop which stocked all the Arnie Palmer and Ben Sherman shirts. Other places included Mr Six Togs and John Hargreaves' place the Hurdy Gurdy Man."

As well as running a clothes shop for a while, John Hargreaves had also been an art teacher at Chesterfield School. The establishment was run on disciplinarian public school lines and many of the 'old school' teachers reflected that, wearing full black gowns and sometimes even mortar boards.

Hargreaves was one of the first of a new, younger breed of tutor to show up at the school to clearly abandon the authoritarian stance and meet students on a more equal footing. Dressing in the 'modern idiom' and making occasional brave attempts at jazz trumpet further established his reputation as a cool beatnik bohemian who was down with the kids.

Back to Pete: "I think it was a Sheffield trip if you wanted anything special and for shoes, Nottingham of course. My mum gave me some money to go and get some school shoes from Nottingham.

Derek Murray and I went, decided we needed a swift drink. 3 hours later we'd spent all the money. Mum wasn't happy."

Al Tagg: "The next step in being a mod was to get a scooter. In those days you could get a provisional licence at the age of 16. So, in my case, that would be in July 1969. To raise enough money for a scooter I got a Saturday job at the Co-op dairy on Chatsworth Road as a milk man. I helped out on the Inkersall, Duckmanton, Poolsbrook milk round.

"After several weeks I discovered that my driver had a scooter in his shed that he hadn't used for ages. He agreed to sell it to me for a very reasonable price. So there I was – now the owner of a Lambretta TV 200. About as good as scooters go. I was made up.

"It was very standard so gave me the opportunity to customise it as I wanted. I had always been interested in engines and racing so although I wanted it to be 'cool' I didn't want it to be over burdened with a million mirrors.

"So a flyscreen, two handlebar mirrors, a back rack with spare wheel with a huge chrome hub cap off a bus, a KL backrest for the pillion a chequered flag rear mudflap and a long chrome megaphone exhaust did the trick.

"The place to park up and hang out on Saturday afternoon was behind the Burlington Grill on a small triangle of pavement in the corner next to the Crooked Spire. Here we would check out each others scooters and generally get together.

King Mojo concerts featuring acts like the Small Faces and Stevie Wonder were a big draw for mod audiences.

The Marquis of Granby – a Peak District destination for mods and their scooters.

"I don't remember many names of the other scooter owners, but there was Jimmy O'Neil, Alan Redpath, Tony Brown, John Bradshaw and a black guy called Del. We would go off on ride-outs to various discos – The Marquis of Grandby near Hathersage, the Olde English in Matlock, some place in Nottingham.

"One night coming back from the Marquis of Granby with Pete Coleman as pillion I managed to crash on a bend between FoxHouse and Owler Bar. I ended up going to hospital to have my face stitched up (open face helmets then) and Pete cut his legs up. On another occasion I remember John Bradshaw crashing coming down Cordwell Valley.

On a Saturday afternoon, then the High Street was open to traffic, so we would ride round and round. Down the High Street to the Market Place, up Glumangate, along Knifesmithgate and back down the High Street. Basically trying to look cool.

"I don't think the police liked this much and we were always being stopped and given tickets to produce our documents at the police station. It became a bit of a competition to see who could get the most tickets.

"There was a bit of Mods v Rockers action in town. A load of rockers used to drive around town in an old Ford Popular on Saturday nights past the Vic and shout abuse at any Mods standing outside. I don't remember much fighting though.

"A ride to Skegness on a bank holiday did involve having to run the gauntlet of lots of rockers parked up in a lay-by on the outskirts. They tried to hit us with studded belts and chains as we went past and our pillion passengers would throw bricks at them, which we had picked up from a local building site. Luckily nobody got hurt.

"So 1969 went by and slid into the seventies. I was now 17 and old enough to drive a car. So I passed my driving test, bought a cheap Mini, and let my hair grow long and turned into a 'weirdo' or 'magic' in the process. But that's another story altogether.

Thought to be taken in 1966, these pics have popped up frequently on social media. According to hazy recollections in Facebook posts, the main pic with the lads on their scooters probably shows (l-r): Kay Bingham, Keith Barker, Graham Bull, Stan Martin and John Watts. Or is one of them Dek Roberts? Their allegiance to Chesterfield is made clear by the town's name featuring proudly on both scooter flyscreens. Apparently John Watts was so skint he bought his petrol by the pint. The pic was taken by Elvin Barker near where Wilcos now stands.

A NIGHT OF BUXTON BLUES

Born to be wild? John Ashforth's pic shows concert goers making their way to the first open air festival in the hills above Buxton in 1972 featuring Steppenwolf, Wishbone Ash and Family. Slade and Curved Air were billed but didn't play.

On a chilly September night in 1969 three likely teenage lads from Chesterfield were probably as excited as they had ever been. Because for the first time in their lives they were being allowed to stay out (and up) all night. Yes, as kids of 14 and 15 they had been given the green light to be hippies for the night at a Progressive Blues Festival at the Pavilion Gardens in Buxton.

Tom Bailey was one of them: "I often find myself theorising about how the music which provides the soundtrack to our coming of age becomes the playlist of an eternal nostalgia. Whatever was coming out of the speakers when we first experimented with sex, drugs and rock'n'roll is forever fixed in the memory.

"This was tantalisingly different: a chance to participate, wide-eyed, in the festivities of the 'permissive' society. "

"The Buxton Festival definitely holds a place in my memory, partly because of the extraordinary talent on stage, but also because it was the first time my friends, Paul Hobday and Pete Dodd and I had stayed out all night without parental supervision. We were just 14 or15 and although there had been sleepovers at friends' homes, there had always been an adult to keep an eye on things.

"This was tantalisingly different: a chance to participate, wide-eyed, in the festivities of the 'permissive' society. I must disappoint immediately by confessing that, in the event, there was no sex or drugs consumed. But there was plenty of rock'n'roll.

"The main event took place in the great chamber of the Buxton Pavilion. On arrival, we pushed to the front, taking our places amongst the cross-legged and supine punters. The fashions of hippie culture and Carnaby Street which had percolated north from London were in sufficient concentration to create a seeming carpet of long hair, tie-died cottons and crushed velvet. The mixed scents of beer, patchouli oil and Players No.6 filled the air.

"The first band I remember seeing was The Spirit of John Morgan, who performed their version of Graham Bond's "*I Want You*". It seemed a signature sign of the times that many of these bands featured the Hammond organ as a lead instrument.

"The same instrumentation was evident in Glass Menagerie. They gave us a version of Dylan's *All Along the Watchtower*, dedicating it to 'you, Bob, wherever you are'. This at least evoked a sense of connectivity with the international counter-culture.

"East of Eden was familiar to us because they had played at least once at the Victoria Ballrooms in Chesterfield. On that occasion, by helping the band carry their equipment up the stairs, Pete and I had snuck in free of charge before the box office opened.

"Falling into conversation with their drummer, Stuart Rossiter, I was impressed with his commitment to whole foods – the first time I had encountered this idea.

"But at the Buxton gig, highlights were provided by frontman Dave Arbus who not only performed their hit "Jig-a-Jig" on violin, but also played two saxophones at once a la Rahsaan Roland Kirk.

Out Demons Out! So said the Edgar Broughton Band who shared the bill with Family and Peter Green's Fleetwood Mac.

"The Edgar Broughton band, a legendary power three-piece which seemed to anticipate ZZ Top with its beards as well as its style of playing, came close to bringing the house down with a song designed to get everyone chanting the words 'Out, Demons, out!'. It was explained as a kind of exorcism, but offered up as a collective rebellion against the status quo.

"It has to be said that these were days when the power of alternative music as an agent of social change was at a seductive peak. Rock'n'roll had become the uncontrollable vehicle of rebellion and an insistent alternative to 'straight' culture. And, in it's symbolism, it seemed somehow that the longer the hair, the louder the guitar, the better the world would become. I don't know if anyone listens to that song now, but at the time it seemed like incitement to revolution pure and powerful.

"Next up, after what I recall was a long break, were Family. They had already secured a reputation as masters of the folk-tinged alternative rock genre, with multi-instrumental additions of flute and violin to the standard line-up. What really impressed the crowd, though, was singer Roger Chapman who, with an almost scarily self-possessed energy, danced mesmerically, stared maniacally and thrashed tambourines to splinters against a mic stand as he performed songs like 'Observations From a Hill' in his characteristic 'Larry the Lamb' voice. As the saying goes, by the end, there was blood on the floor – literally, in this case.

Edgar Broughton Band

Family

"The festival headliners were Fleetwood Mac. Their mega-hit, *Albatross* had recently caught the imagination of the nation, so they were probably the only group of the night to have been on BBC's Top of the Pops. But their deserved reputation as princes of the British blues explosion preceded them.

Fleetwood Mac

"Three guitar heroes: Peter Green, "Mississippi" Jeremy Spencer and Danny Kirwan, formed the frontline, while the rhythm section which gave the band it's name: Mick Fleetwood and John McVie, held it all together very convincingly.

"I remember that Fleetwood took to the stage with the same wooden balls hanging from his belt which were to appear years later on the cover photograph of their enormously successful album *Rumours*. By then, of course, all three legendary guitarists had left, so I feel lucky to have seen them in this early incarnation. They opened their set with *Shake Your Money Maker* and Green also sang the blues classic *It Hurts Me*, Too before satisfying the anticipation of everyone there with a lengthy version of *Albatross*. The concert was also used to debut their future hit *Oh Well*.

"By around 5am we were all hungry, exhausted and cramped. I remember thoughtlessly asking compere John Peel if we could sit on the side of the stage to stretch our legs."

"By around 5am we were all hungry, exhausted and cramped. I remember thoughtlessly asking compere John Peel if we could sit on the side of the stage to stretch our legs. He sensibly refused. Rumours of naked capers in the Pavilion Gardens

Poster promoting the 1969 Buxton Progressive

By the following year price of entry had gone up by half a crown.

teased us away from the stage, but proved to be unreliable. And suddenly, it was all over. I don't remember anything about the journey home. I was probably asleep."

Tom and his crew never ventured away from the main stage in the Pavilion but there was a second stage at the neighbouring Playhouse Theatre where Chesterfield's (or indeed Eckington's) Shape of the Rain delivered a set. Also listed were Grisby Dyke, Jugular Vein and some poets.

At the Buxton All Night Festival a year later Richard Knight slept through Savoy Brown:

"But I was ecstatic at Rory Gallagher's Taste. Here was the real deal. Rick Wakeman did a satin-caped cabaret. I nodded off again."

To cater for bigger crowds, promoter Stephen Robinson began to stage open air festivals in the Derbyshire hills above Buxton. They were often blighted by truly dreadful weather.

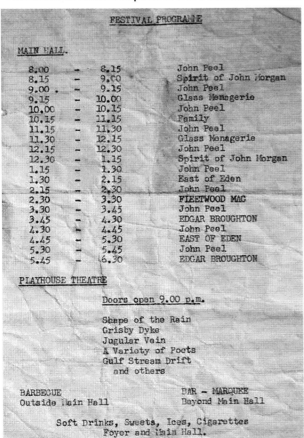

Left: A typed out running order for the concert, starting at 8pm and running to 6.30am the following morning.

CHAPTER 9

...AND 50 YEARS OF **FOLK**

Bold Rodney, previously Celtic Cross, were regulars at Stainsby.
Here they are at one of the earlier festivals (l-r): brothers Paul and Pat
Gambles, Paul Hague, Mark Jinkinson, Chris Drew and Pete Dodd. And
bottom of the bill on a Stainsby flyer.]

STAINSBY
FOLK FESTIVAL
August 26, 27 & 28

GUESTS - Shirley and Dolly Collins
Tannahill Weavers + Bully wee
Hedgehog Pie + Threadbare
John James + Kempion + John Coy
Packie Byrne and Bonnie Shaljean
Robin Garside and Paul Gough
Bernie Parry + Bob Chiswick
George Deacon and Marion Ross
John Leonard and John Squire
Jiggery Polkary Ceilidh Band
Mogs Marvels Ceilidh Band
Tom Brown + Pat Ryan
Tony Capstick
Bold Rodney

MAKE STAINSBY YOUR BANK HOLIDAY WEEKEND

In the summer of 2018, Stainsby Festival celebrated its 50th anniversary. It has come a long way since its inception in 1969 and now has a unique claim in the annals of music festival history – it is a year older than Glastonbury and has never dropped a year!

Festival Chairman Tony Trafford has been around pretty much since the beginning and explains how it all came about: "It was the Stainsby Arts Project basically. The schoolhouse in the village became redundant when the secondary school that was here moved to its new building in Heath in around 1963. It was taken over by the Youth Service who weren't quite sure what to do with it and they eventually decided, with it being the sixties, that some arts provision was needed and that's how the arts centre came about starting in 1966."

It was a place for film screenings (your author remembers seeing Eisenstein's *Battleship Potemkin* there on a school trip) and theatre productions and it involved young people from the area mainly from Doe Lea and Bramley Vale.

Tony: "Bob Walker from the East Midlands Folk Federation and Ann Syrett, who was running the arts festival, suggested putting on a weekend folk festival as part of the events in the summer of 1969. Steeleye Span and Dave Swarbrick were among the performers.

Tony: "It was a real hand-to-mouth thing involving the village providing a cart for a stage and hay bales for people to sit on and a lot of late teenage kids from Doe Lea helped put it on. Everyone had a rather good time, or rather they were told they had afterwards, as it was the 1960s. They decided they really wanted to keep doing it. It kind of just grew from there really.

"It got bigger but it was an awful site for it in some ways with the beer tent at the top of the field and the performance marquee down at the bottom. By the time you got back to the marquee with your beer you'd spilt most of it and needed to go again."

Separate entrances for the girls and boys.

Folk fans gathering in the old Stainsby school yard.

The old Stainsby School House featuring the steep grassy bank that made manual beer transportation a hazardous activity.

In 1973 Stainsby gained a certain notoriety when it won the *Melody Maker* award for 'worst bogs at any festival'.

When Bob Walker moved into politics Dave Davidson of the Springbank Youth Centre in Chesterfield took over running the festival. This is probably why young Chesterfield Irish-influenced folk band Bold Rodney (previously Celtic Cross) performed at Stainsby quite a few times – they were based at Springbank and Dave Davidson was very supportive.

Disaster nearly struck when the school building and surrounding land was leased by the National Trust to a boys' Catholic school from Bradford which didn't take to the idea of hosting a folk festival and pulled the plug on the 1975 event.

In 1973 Stainsby gained a certain notoriety when it won the *Melody Maker* award for 'worst bogs at any festival'.

To the rescue came local landowner Dot Brunt who offered the use of her fields at nearby Brunt's Farm where the festival continues to be held to this day. It is this swift recovery, led by Brenda Whitmore and Ken Blankley, that gives Stainsby its unique claim over Glastonbury.

Tony confesses that in the early days he had absolutely no idea it would become such an institution: "It's run on a voluntary basis and people get absorbed into the fabric: It's one of those organisations that's porous. People come and start doing stuff and when you are in a volunteer-run organisation, a volunteer that wants to work is very welcome.

"As an organisation we suck people in and they take ownership of it – that's probably one of the reasons it has lasted. It only happens because you do what you do – it's an investment and you get a lot of effort out of people to keep it going.

Stainsby Girls

For Robi Qazi as she was then, it was always a frustration that she was too young to go to the major festivals in the sixties. They seemed to herald the age of the teenager – young people who were establishing a recognised place in society by developing their own culture, displayed most notably through clothes and music.

So although all the major festivals of the 1960s were to elude her, there was always Stainsby Folk Festival just on the outskirts of Chesterfield to give her a sense of what she had been missing at bigger events elsewhere.

Robi: "I moved to Chesterfield in 1969 aged 14 and persuaded my parents that everyone I knew was going to this event on the far side of Heath roundabout and that I must go too.

"My major concern and consideration was to wear the right clothes. Having never been to a festival before it was somewhat a stab in the dark. My only reference point was *Jackie* magazine.

"Suffering the slightly sick making bus ride from Elder Way to Sheffield I went to C&A. Modern clothing at affordable prices. I bought a long

June Tabor

Steeleye Span

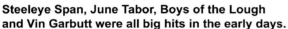

Steeleye Span, June Tabor, Boys of the Lough and Vin Garbutt were all big hits in the early days.

Above: Vin Garbutt

Right: Boys of the : Lough

Robi Qazi has her own recollections of an early Stainsby – but the music wasn't high on the agenda.

sleeved cream T-shirt with a huge butterfly on the front in various shades of blue & purple. I thought it looked appropriately hippy and alternative enough and teamed with jeans I just might look like a seasoned festival goer.

"Surprisingly the outfit seemed to work, I was chatted up by an older boy within an hour of arriving and spent most of my time with him. He called me Miss Butterfly, after my T-shirt.

"A field sloped down from the school house to the stage. The weather was fine and I spent much of the day lounging on this grassy hill chatting to the boy. I don't actually remember much about the music.

"I do remember thinking I had had a great time and liked the fact that when my dad came to pick me up, his car headlights caught me kissing the boy goodbye. Was I being a rebellious teenager? I thought my dad might say something about kissing strange boys but all he asked was had I had a good time? Bless him."

Iris Gaunt's association with Stainsby became life long: "At the end of the sixties there was a rumour of a folk festival to be held in the tiny hamlet of Stainsby. Alas, I had no idea where Stainsby was, so I didn't go.

"Having heard later how good the atmosphere had been, I did track it down in its second year. As fate would have it, I have now lived in Stainsby for 30 years and this year (2018)

have just enjoyed Stainsby's 50th birthday celebration."

And as a local she got a free pass to the vice presidents' celebratory evening on the Thursday night before the music began on the Friday.

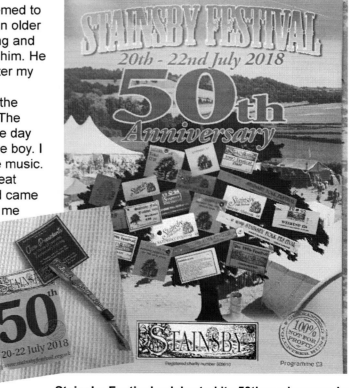

Stainsby Festival celebrated its 50th anniversary in 2018 and produced a bumper full colour programme to prove it (reproduced here in lavish monochrome). Being a resident of the tiny village Iris Gaunt was invited to the Vice Presidents' celebratory evening to mark the festival's half century.

A **ROSE** BY ANY OTHER NAME

In the case of Geraldine Rose, that other name was McPhie. At the start of the 1960s Geraldine was, in her own words, "an unremarkable girl of 13". She had not a single responsibility in her world other than studying for GCEs. But by the end of that decade she was a married mother and a partner in an exciting music shop business. Her husband was David McPhie.

Geraldine provides a welcome woman's perspective on life in the 1960s and frames it against the politics of the day.

Geraldine: "After leaving school at 16 I was nursing for three years at Chesterfield Royal Hospital studying to be an SRN. After that I worked in Robinson's factory for five months, cutting out PVC shapes for babies paddy pants, then at the AGD (head Post Office) as a clerical officer, in the Market Hall on Cannon's Crockery Stall and as a waitress at the Bernie Inn Steak Bar. My goodness, it was so easy to get jobs in those days!

"Before the birth of my baby girl, I had also opened up a record shop in partnership with David. We then lived above the shop on the corner of Newbold Road

"The hospital was run by mostly 'immigrant' doctors and nurses and I can't imagine how it would have been possible to keep going without them but even so it was whilst working in the hospital that I first came across any form of racism.

"I went for my break from the ward with a friend, Shirley. Amongst other things, we had been making beds all morning together. A white British girl in the same year as me called me over to the table where she and others were sitting and asked why I was sitting with 'them'.

"It took me a while to understand her meaning because in Bolsover, where I grew up, I had never experienced racism – we were just all, mainly, poor together. She meant, why was I sitting at the same table as Nigerian and Jamaican nurses of course. I was both horrified and amazed that a

Geraldine, on the left, as a student nurse on Basil Ward, Christmas 1964.

nurse could think in those terms."

When Geraldine left nursing in 1967 she applied for a job, sat the exams and was interviewed by the board at Red House, a retirement home on Sheffield Road, for the post of Assistant Matron. She got the job but was about to marry and when she learnt that it was a 'live-in' job so she had to turn it down.

Geraldine: "I married whilst still a teenager and just over two years' later I gave birth to my daughter, Louisa. I was 22. David and I first lived in a rented flat behind a grocer's shop on Chatsworth Road when we married in 1967, and it was there where we recorded Joe Cocker's first demo disc. We took to London to the record promoter, Tony Hall.

David had been managing Joe for a while, booking him into venues like 'The Barrow Hill Hotel' for £10 a night, but with a voice like his we knew he was destined for bigger things!

(Mick Twelves' band King Mob Echo played support to Joe Cocker at the Magic Village in Manchester in 1969: "Backstage there was the last time I saw him in person, and what a lovely guy. RIP."

"Before the birth of my baby girl, I had also opened up a record shop in partnership with David. We then lived above the shop on the corner of Newbold Road, near where it intersects with Sheffield Road. The shop was called 'Some

Geraldine's first date with David was at Peter Stringfellow's Mojo Club in Sheffield. Ike and Tina Turner were the star turn.

Kinda Mushroom', a lyric taken from the song *White Rabbit* by Jefferson Airplane (based on Lewis Carrol's *Alice in Wonderland*).

April 4, 1967 – Right: Geraldine and David's wedding day made national headlines when 'the groom wore white'.

"We married in Chesterfield Registry Office, that was then located on Newbold Road and the nurses on duty in Scarsdale Hospital hung out the windows and cheered. We had wanted a small wedding without fuss but someone had tipped off the *Sheffield Star* the evening before and hundreds of young people turned up to see Chesterfield's DJ, who ran many clubs, including the Locomotion and the Velvet Underground on two floors at the Victoria Ballroom.

"The headline in the *Sun* newspaper (they must have picked it up from the local press) read "And the Groom Wore White" (well before John Lennon did the same in March 1969!). A photograph of David lifting me up exposed my 'pants' from my white mini dress and matching pant outfit (bought from C&A for £5). In the background the nurses in Scarsdale were waving through the window. My plain white gold wedding ring was £10 and the most expensive item in the cost of our marriage.

"Managing bands and trips to London to recording studios with Shape of the Rain became our way of life until I gave birth to Louisa. We stayed with Tony Hall, who had a column in the Melody Maker and promoted such people as Dusty Springfield at the time. Although firmly against apartheid, Dusty agreed to visit South Africa in 1964 on condition she wouldn't perform in front of segregated audiences. She was deported back to Britain!

"We got to know Tony Hall when we took Joe Cocker's demo disc to him (recorded in our front room, in a flat behind a grocery shop on Chatsworth Road, with just an eight track mixer).

"Joe played most of the instruments, apart from guitar which was played by Chris Stainton (of the Greasband). Tony Hall was knocked out by Joe's voice. Later we took a demo disc of Shape of the Rain (a local band David managed). We spent a lot of time in recording studios and London Clubs around that time, when I was heavily pregnant with Louisa, and Tony insisted we stay the night with them. I remember being impressed by the fresh, crisp, white bed-linen!

"David and I ran a club above the Red Lion on Vicar Lane for a while playing US imported 'soul' music that attracted mostly mods. It was called 'Club Harlem'..."

"David and I ran a club above the Red Lion on Vicar Lane for a while playing US imported 'soul' music that attracted mostly mods. It was called 'Club Harlem', I seem to recall. Or was it 'The Locomotion'? I was on the door and occasionally there would be scuffles between rival factions downstairs on the street."

Geraldine made a dress for her first date with David – a blue velvet empire-line dress that fell to

the floor: "I bought the material from a Chesterfield market stall and stitched it all by hand – I didn't have a sewing machine! David was taking me to the Mojo in Sheffield, where I'd never been before.

"Whilst we were talking to Pete Stringfellow, he commented on my dress – I was really pleased with myself as it was the first dress that I had made! Ike and Tina Turner and the Ikettes were playing that night – Tina was amazing. Who knew then how she was being abused by Ike?

"I remember the night well because of that dress. I had to hoist it up under my hospital gaberdine (the only coat I had) so that it couldn't be seen on the bus journey from Bolsover to Vicar Lane in Chesterfield where David was picking me up in his car. Obviously long dresses were not yet that commonplace. I was just pleased that it didn't fall to pieces on the dance floor!

"Psychedelic music had a massive impact on the sixties: the Beatles' *Sgt Pepper's Lonely Hearts Club Band* was released in 1967, and other albums out around this time included Jimi Hendrix's *Are You Experienced?*, Cream's *Disraeli Gears* and Pink Floyd's *The Piper at the Gates of*

""Whilst we were talking to Pete Stringfellow, he commented on my dress – I was really pleased with myself as it was the first dress that I had made! "

Dawn. Jazz Expo '69 at the Hammersmith Odeon, from October 25 to November 1, was an event I'll never forget.

(The event which took place at the Royal Festival Hall as well as the Hammersmith Odeon was billed as 'The Newport Jazz Festival in London' and performers included Miles Davis, Wayne Shorter, Chick Corea, Mary Lou Williams, Thelonious Monk, Sarah Vaughan, Cecil Taylor, John Lee Hooker, Champion Jack Dupree, Otis Spann, Albert King, Lionel Hampton, Teddy Wilson, Bill Coleman, Albert Nicholas, Gary Burton, Kenny Clarke, Francy Boland, and many more.)

"We stayed with Dick, the brother of our friend and guitarist, Jeff Pountain (From David's band The Blueberries). We slept on a mattress on the floor of Dick's room. Dick was a student at the time and he shared a house with a load of other boys in Notting Hill.

"In the evenings we saw blues legends such as Sun House, Skip James, Sonny Terry and Brownie Magee, John Lee Hooker, Champion Jack Dupree, Otis Spann and Albert King. I remember wandering around the house one morning and came across two boys working on a cartoon animation. They said it was for a film to be called *Yellow Submarine*.

Above: Mick Twelves, with his Afro hairstyle on Shaftesbury Avenue with (l-r): Geraldine, her mum, her sister holding Mick's baby Rhys and her daughter Louisa.

Kitchen Sink Drama
In the late 1950s and early 1960s 'kitchen sink' dramas emerged in theatre, novels, film, and as television plays. It used a style of social realism, which depicted the often tough domestic situations of working class Britons, to explore challenging social and political issues.

Geraldine: "For me it was too close to real life. I saw 'Cathy Come Home' and although it was an excellent film and did raise awareness at the time, if truthful, I preferred escapism, like science fiction. Glamour and magic wasn't part of our every day lives growing up in Bolsover.

"We sold imported American bootleg LPs as well as IT and 'under the counter' magazines, like *Oz*, which was considered 'obscene' at the time by some and resulted in the famous *Oz* obscenity trial of 1971 over issue no. 28, the notorious *Schoolkids OZ*, which famously featured an adaptation by Vivian Berger of a Robert Crumb cartoon which featured Rupert Bear in an explicitly sexual situation.

"The magazine regularly enraged the British Establishment with a range of left-field stories including heavy critical coverage of the Vietnam War and the anti-war movement, discussions of drugs, sex and alternative lifestyles, and contentious political stories, such as the magazine's revelations about the torture of citizens under the rule of the military junta in Greece."

A Council House and Cannabis
With another baby on the way Geraldine applied for a council house: "We got one in Newbold on Lancaster Road just before the birth of my second child, Jamie. That was another thing that was relatively easy to get in those days – a council house.

"Inevitably, the shop was regularly full of musicians, just hanging around. As we were not living over the shop any more I decided that I might as well open a coffee bar upstairs. It ended up being a doss-house for cannabis smokers and I was afraid we would get closed down so I stopped baking cakes and making coffee and closed the cafe.

"Inevitably, the shop was regularly full of musicians, just hanging around. As we were not living over the shop any more I decided that I might as well open a coffee bar upstairs."

"We eventually bought a house on Shaftesbury Avenue in Ashgate, opposite the home of Peggy Dodd and her son, Pete. Our children were small and we always seemed to have most of the kids on the street playing in our garden. We often had some homeless person living with us in those days, mostly my sister with friends she had collected on her travels.

"David's brother, Paul, lived with us for a while and Mick Twelves, as a single father with his baby boy, Rhys, who I looked after during the day whilst Mick worked in the record shop. When I was also working we left Rhys with my sister or my friend, Jean, or my mum.

"Around that time Mick and I used to sell records on market stalls on a Saturday, sometimes in the snow! We drove all over the place queuing up for a stall. We didn't always get one so had to drive to another town and try again! Those were the days!

After A Fashion

Although she makes no claims to being a fashionista herself, Geraldine can't really talk about the sixties without mentioning the clothes – even in Chesterfield!: "It was a decade that broke many fashion traditions, mirroring social movements during the time.

"The sixties saw the emergence of the Mod movement, which took inspiration from trendy high fashion European designers. The look was well-tailored, with clean lines. Mods rode scooters (probably to keep their clothes tidy) and 'rockers' rode motorbikes and sported long hair and studded leather jackets.

"Popular models of the time were Twiggy and Jean Shrimpton – obviously Twiggy got her name from her characteristic skinny legs 'look' and the

Geraldine and David's flat on Chatsworth Road at the bottom of Schoolboard Lane. A Joe Cocker demo disc was recorded in the front room. Palfreyman's Music shop is now on the corner.

60

beginning of the look that was maybe responsible for much of the trend that followed. She was the face of 1966.

"Still, women are continuing to battle on a daily basis with eating disorders, suffering from depression trying to make themselves thinner, aspiring to have the look of Twiggy, for many an impossible ideal. Twiggy has admitted she wasn't that happy with the way she looked in the sixties but couldn't help it as she had a small frame and small boobs and although she ate lots she obviously had a metabolism that enabled her skinniness.

"The 1960s featured a number of diverse trends including the mini skirt. However, apart from my wedding day, I usually wore long skirts – this style was beginning to be popular with the advent of hippies and music festivals and 'wearing flowers in your hair' (in San Fransisco at least), but I like to think that I simply preferred long skirts, or maybe it was really because I didn't want to expose my legs!

The Times They Are A Changin'

Geraldine: "In the sixties Bob Dylan sang, *The Times They Are a Changin'* and we hoped that they were. But now, nearly five decades later, I would say that the change that we had hoped to see has not been achieved. Popular dystopian authors wrote about this future in which we are now living: George Orwell's 1944 novel: 'Nineteen Eighty Four' was prophetic. My son, Jamie, wrote recently about this dystopia by articulating that: 'We are now stuck in 1984. We are living in the dystopian future of the past 30 years. Orwell's 1984 has already happened but we seem to have become numb to it, baffled by the shiny lights of neoliberal capitalism and its henchman, globalisation'.

"The sixties were dominated by the Vietnam War, Civil Rights Protests, the assassinations of US President John F Kennedy and activist Martin Luther King, the Cuban Missile Crisis and finally the first person landing on the moon, whilst at the same time the world saw hunger and poverty on a massive scale as capitalism exploded.

"I'd been on holiday in France, staying with a 'pen-friend' (do they still have such things, I wonder, in this age of social media, internet?) and we spent a few days in Paris. This was in 1964 – four years later there would be the Paris Riots of May, 1968, the fore-runner to the student uprisings in San Francisco, and the 'Summer of Love'.

Antoine Guégan, 27, was part of the Censier campus student takeover that was raided by police in May this year (2018). His father, Gérard Guégan, staged sit-ins at the same campus, aged 27, in May 1968. Antoine Guégan, said: "If there's one thing in common between 1968 and today, it's

David and Geraldine ran a club above the Red Lion on Vicar Lane for a while playing US soul imports that attracted mostly mods. It was Club Harlem – or was it The Locomotion, wonders Geraldine?

young people's despair. But it's a different kind of despair, because the social and economic context is not the same. In 1968, there was a global movement, there was rock music, new sexual freedom, a different culture and a desire to change the old world."

"Things were going to be different. We thought there would be no more wars! I didn't realise the importance of what was happening at the time

> **"Things were going to be different. We thought there would be no more wars! I didn't realise the importance of what was happening at the time – we were only students but thought that we could change society for the better. "**

– we were only students but thought that we could change society for the better.

"I remember sitting on the steps of the Sacré-Cœur in Montmartre, along with many other students, singing The *Times They Are a Changin'*, and other freedom songs. At the beginning of the 1960s, many believed they were standing at the dawn of a golden age but by the end of the decade we saw that the golden age had never materialised, at least not in the way that it was envisioned by many.

"In the summer of 1969 more than 400,000 young people attended the Woodstock Music Festival in upstate New York, a harmonious three days that seemed to represent the best of the peace-and-love generation. But the era's legacy remains mixed – it brought us empowerment and polarisation, resentment and liberation – but it has certainly become a permanent part of our political and cultural history.

CHAPTER 11

THE SIGNIFICANCE OF THE CINEMA

ABC Regal interior.

T he decade became a journey from dull greys to full colour. The 1963 film *Summer Holiday* starring Cliff Richard can be cited as an early and inadvertent summing up the 1960s trajectory from grim austerity to the summer of love. The story focuses on Don (Cliff Richard) and his young chums who work as bus mechanics at a London Transport depot in Hertfordshire.

Like the sixties themselves, the movie starts out in drab black and white until the bus swings around the corner, then the movie bursts into vibrant full colour.

To escape the relentless dreariness of a wet British summer, Don persuades London Transport to lend him and his friends a big red double-decker bus in which to embark on a romantic adventure across mainland Europe. Like the sixties themselves, the movie starts out in drab black and white until the bus swings around the corner, then the movie bursts into vibrant full colour. For a young person like me who longed at the time for technicolor over old-fashioned monochrome,

ABC Logo

(unconcerned with the marvels of art house cinema), this was a great production 'trick'.

Also the two live action Beatles' films, *A Hard Day's Night* and *Help!*, managed to convey a similar development. Released in 1964, *A Hard Day's Night* was domestic and Blighty-bound, shot in gritty monochrome and was concerned with hordes of screaming fans and Paul McCartney's rather unpleasant grandfather John (Wilfred Brambell).

Just two years later *Help!* is a multicoloured extravaganza seeing the Fab Four visit exotic locations including the Austrian alps and the Bahamas with a plot following an eastern cult prepared to go to any lengths to retrieve a ring stuck on Ringo's finger.

Suffice to say, the Beatles' next film, the animated Yellow Submarine, arrived in 1968 after flower power had fully blossomed and was a celebration of full-blown lysergic psychedelia.

All these films attracted large crowds in Chesterfield. As the decade dawned there were three picture houses in the centre of Chesterfield, The Gaumont located in the Victoria Ballroom complex succumbed to bingo in 1965, closing on January 30, 1965 with Albert Finney in *Tom Jones*. But the ABC Regal and the Odeon would continue to serve up filmed entertainment for the whole of the decade.

The ABC Regal, Cavendish Street.

The ABC

By far the most culturally significant cinema for me was the ABC on Cavendish Street. It was there one night, emerging from the cinema as a young lad with his father, that I had my first brush with celebrity.

My dad had taken me to see some Western or an 007-style spy drama and as we stepped out into the dark night he suddenly struck up an animated conversation with a tall, dark, handsome young stranger walking past the cinema with his glamorous girlfriend. It was Dronfield's finest Dave Berry who shot to stardom in 1964 with the Top 5 hit *The Crying Game*.

My dad was a reporter on the *Derbyshire Times* and, as it transpired that night, he was one of the first journalists to give Berry some exposure in the press as he stepped out on his chart bound journey. Hence the convivial banter and a son's proud realisation that his dad knew famous people!

The ABC Minors

"We are the boys and girls
well known as minors of the ABC
And every Saturday all line up, to see the films
we like and shout aloud with glee.
We love to laugh and have our sing song, such
a happy crowd are we.
We're all pals together, the minors of the ABC."

But it was a more permanent association with the Regal cinema that cemented it as a place of significance – the Saturday morning flicks. For many junior and early senior school kids it was their first experience of stepping out on the town free from parental interference.

This 'grown-up' trip to the cinema was of course preceded by a visit to Mr. Bell's sweetshop opposite the picture house. Butterscotch gums, coconut mushrooms, sherbet fountains, bubble gum and many more delights were on the menu.

ABC minors' badges, made ultra groovy by the fact they were glow-in-the-dark luminous.

ABC Minors glued to the screen.

And then to the cinema itself for a visual diet of Warner Bros Merrie Melodies cartoons (featuring such legends as *Bugs Bunny, Foghorn Leghorn, Tweety Pie, Sylvester, Speedy Gonzales, Roadrunner* and *Yosemite Sam*).

Also on offer was the cliffhanger serial whose nail-biting endings often seemed rather less nail-biting when resolved at the start of the following week's episode.

To finish off the morning there was usually a mini-feature aimed direct at the children's market. Many of these were produced by the Children's Film Foundation (CFF) which was set up in 1951 to make films specifically for children to be screened at Saturday morning matinees and used in schools.

Also on offer was the cliffhanger serial whose nail-biting endings often seemed rather less nail-biting when resolved at the start of the following week's episode.

Support from the British film industry enabled the Foundation to make five or six low budget films a year. They were enjoyed by many and gave a leg up to some child actors who would later become household names, such as Francesca Annis, Michael Crawford and Dennis Waterman.

Package Tours

But the real significance of the ABC, for me, was that it hosted the 1960s package tours, which brought charting singers and groups all the way from London to your hometown. I would still have been an ABC Minor when I started attending these and, thus, it was the first significant live music I would experience as a kid was in Chesterfield in the mid-1960s.

As previously stated, my dad worked at the Derbyshire Times and as a result could get free entry to the pop package tours that pitched up in town every few months. So as a child barely into double figures I experienced the delights of

The Children's Film Foundation made features especially for Saturday morning cinema. One of them, Operation Third Form from 1966, follows the exploits of young schoolboy Dick whose night in a nearly abandoned school building leads to a broken window, a scenario with a scary skeleton, and false accusations of stealing a valuable bell from the HMS Dolphin. Actor Derren Nesbitt plays a villain named Skinner who is pictured here (entirely coincidentally as it's set in north London) with a company called Chesterfield Motors behind him.

Above: Jimi, Cat, Gary Leeds and Eng backstage during the 1967 tour.
Right: The penultimate ABC package show featuring Hendrix and Humperdinck on the same bill.

artistes such as Cliff Richard (more than once!), Billy Fury, Adam Faith, The Searchers and Patsy Anne Noble, who seemed (to quote Jeff Beck) to be everywhere and nowhere, baby, all at the same time. As ubiquitous as she was, to me, obscure.

Overall, I was not particularly impressed. My dad said he could arrange it for me to meet the stars backstage, but even at that tender age I intuitively declined an audience with Cliff – and everybody else.

With the Beatles and the Stones already emerging, these acts were simply old hat to a youngster with no concept of historical context. I was living in the now – the Mop Tops had arrived, Elvis was a chubby has-been and psychedelia and the Summer of Love were just around the corner.

Even the legendary Everly Brothers, who performed at the ABC on October 27, 1965 – my 12th birthday, got tarred with the same has-been brush. But as the decade progressed so did the package acts.

As mentioned elsewhere, by the time I was 13 I'd started to shell out thirty two shillings and sixpence-a-go on albums, starting with *The Piper at the Gates of Dawn* by Syd Barrett's Pink Floyd,

and followed by the Small Faces' first eponymous album for the Immediate label (brilliant but no hits, although Chris Farlowe had slight success with a cover of *My Way of Giving*.) and Hendrix' *Axis Bold As Love*. All three of these fabulous acts, so crucial to my formative years, I very nearly saw in Chesterfield – but didn't (I did see the Floyd – but, sadly, no Syd).

Before package tours fizzled out altogether they tried a valiant, if doomed, move to keep up with the times, resulting in strange marriages between the likes of Engelbert Humberdinck and Jimi Hendrix on the same bill

Before package tours fizzled out altogether they tried a valiant, if doomed, move to keep up with the times, resulting in strange marriages between the likes of Engelbert Humberdinck and Jimi Hendrix on the same bill (April 1967).

This was a concert that, tragically, I didn't attend and, with hindsight, I detect the censorial

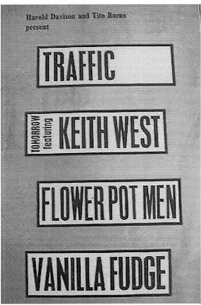

Harold Davison and Tito Burns present

TRAFFIC

TOMORROW featuring **KEITH WEST**

FLOWER POT MEN

VANILLA FUDGE

The last ABC package show of its kind.

intervention of a (needlessly?) concerned mother. I seem to recall my mum describing Hendrix as (something like) lascivious and therefore an unsuitable influence on a young lad's developing mind. That free press ticket just never materialised.

I also missed the Small Faces at the Top Rank (In fact I missed the Top Rank altogether). Surely my mum hadn't latched on to the band's brazen recreational drug references in their high-flying chart sounds? I even missed Syd Barret when the Floyd came to town. In this case, I was there but he wasn't. David Gilmour had just stepped in to replace the troubled Barrett when they played St James' Hall in March, 1969. I was mortified. Not

only was my hero not there but, according to Gilmour to whom we spoke after the concert, it didn't look like he was ever coming back.

Returning to the packages, I did manage to catch a truly psychedelic show (later in 1967 and about the last of its kind) featuring Traffic (first time I saw a sitar in action), The Flowerpot Men (*Let's Go To San Francisco* – dodgy harmonies and cracked falsetto), Tomorrow featuring Keith West (*My White Bicycle* and *Excerpt From a Teenage Opera*), Vanilla

A feature of cinema attendance in those days is once you'd paid to go in you could stay as long as you liked. Now, not everyone would want to bother...

Fudge (who presumably did the rocked up version of *You Keep Me Hanging On*, though I can't remember), and the Mindbenders (*Groovy Kind of Love*).

I definitely saw the Yardbirds (which means I also saw Manfred Mann on the same bill) as I had Jeff Beck's autograph, courtesy of my dad, presumably, or John Dixon the cinema manager who was a neighbour, in a now long-lost autograph book. As I recall it was on the same page as Mr. Pastry.

Carlton Club

The Carlton Cabaret Club, on Duke Street in Whittington Moor was one of the first of its kind outside London's West End in the 1960s and attracted stars such as American singer Johnnie Ray, entertainer Bob Monkhouse, actress Diana Dors and local comedian Bernie Clifton.

The club was developed for ballroom dancing, gambling and dining for the smart suit and posh frock brigade.

Apparently Hendrix played another set there, although Margaret confesses she was more interested in the possibility of securing the *Last Waltz* with Engelbert

According to Margaret Podgorski, an event of particular interest unfolded on the same night that Jimi Hendrix, Engelbert Humperdinck, Cat Stevens and the Walker Brothers all performed on the same bill at the ABC Cinema in town and many of the stars adjourned to the Carlton for some après-gig relaxation.

Apparently Hendrix played another set there, although Margaret confesses she was more interested in the possibility of securing the *Last Waltz* with Engelbert than catching Jimi's psychedelic show.

A regular Carlton DJ was Ken Blair. A friend of David McPhie, Ken was an experienced compère with the Liverpool Cavern on his CV, and a couple of Isle of Wight summer sessions to his name, doing the round of hotels, ballrooms and the odd 'End of the Pier Show' for a living.

According to David, Ken worked for Derek Wright and Johnny Thomas at the Carlton Club on a regular basis: "He had some hair-raising stories to tell of some of the variety/cabaret artists who appeared there, including (the aforementioned) Diana Dors, Les Dawson, and some big visiting American names."

3RD PICTURE HOUSE (NEW WHITTINGTON) c.1930
1820 © Tv Wheatcroft - old chesterfield pics

the 1967 hit *Jungle Book* amongst others. This exotic drama chimed well with the times and seemed so much more relevant than it's fairytale located Disney predecessors like *Sleeping Beauty* and *Snow White*. The film's two showstopping songs *The Bare Necessities* and *I Wanna Be Like You* (sung respectively by Phil Harris and Louis Prima) were performed by decidedly counter culture characters Baloo the bear and King Louie the bonkers orangutan.

As the orphaned man cub Mowgli's self-appointed mentor, the chilled out Baloo advises against a return to the man village in favour of a laid back, carefree existence in the jungle.

Elsewhere crazed hipster and jungle VIP King Louie and his band of dissolute apes want Mowgli to teach them the secret of 'man's real fire'

Unbridled hippiedom.

Elsewhere crazed hipster and jungle VIP King Louie and his band of dissolute apes want Mowgli to teach them the secret of 'man's real fire'. Alas, the king of the swinger's attempts to take a step up the evolutionary ladder results in chaos which reduces his kingdom to rubble.

Kaa the Indian python is similarly 'alternative' as he uses hallucinogenic hypnotism in a bid to devour the lad. As are the down beat and droll barbershop Beatles – a quartet of close harmony vultures who welcome Mowgli as a fellow outcast.

The 'establishment' is represented by Bagheera the fusspot black panther whose guardian role is to return Mowgli to the village, and the shambolic troop of elephants led by Colonel Hathi and his wife Winifred. Even the murderous Bengal tiger Shere Khan, who fancies a slice of man cub on his dinner plate, is voiced by George Sanders and sounds the epitome of an English aristocrat.

On another note entirely, the cinema, now the Winding Wheel concert hall, would later be home to the Jingles and Fusion night clubs.

Left: Syd in the background already looking on his way out in every sense. Gilmour is bottom left.

The Odeon

The Odeon on Holywell Street also had its role to play. Another hidden benefit of having a local journalist father was a 'get in free' card for the Odeon which allowed two people entry each

ODEON

week, an excellent courting device which enabled a fumbling teenager to discover the advantages of the back row of the cinema for hand-holding, snogging (Dear me, do people still do that?) and smoking fags. If a movie was retained 'by popular demand' for a second week, it was possible to see virtually none of the film at all. The balcony tended to be very quiet on weekdays.

A feature of cinema attendance in those days is once you'd paid to go in you could stay as long as you liked. Now, not everyone would want to bother, but if you were particularly keen on a movie you could sit down and watch it in the late afternoon, followed by the inferior support feature, and then watch the main feature all over again. With no fear of being turfed out.

This was the right approach to appreciate

Chesterfield Odeon showing Jungle Book in the late 1960s.

CHAPTER 12

THE ART SCHOOL DANCE GOES ON **FOREVER**

Art school-trained Pete Brown rose to prominence on the London music scene as a lyricist for *Disraeli Gears* era Cream collaborating with Jack Bruce on *I Feel Free, White Room* and *SWLABR*, and with Eric Clapton on *Sunshine of Your Love*.

He was a musician in his own right and the first album release by his band Pete Brown and Piblokto! was called *Things May Come and Things May Go but the Art School Dance Goes On Forever*. The title has probably survived rather better than the contents of the disc, partly perhaps because it was a memorable pointer to the significant part art colleges were playing not just in

fine art and graphics, but increasingly in music as well.

For Chesterfielder John Ashforth the mid-60s was a time of searching that would lead him to art school. He grew up in Hasland in the bosom of the Anglican Church but by his mid-teens he had managed to drop out of school and the church simultaneously. He would eventually find salvation at the local art college. That's where life started to make sense for him for the first time.

John: "Somewhat confused, I was unconsciously looking for meaning in life. I could not have imagined that I would have the opportunity to take part in such enriching, mind deepening

Spot the difference: John Ashforth at Penmore House in Hasland where he studied photography and life itself.

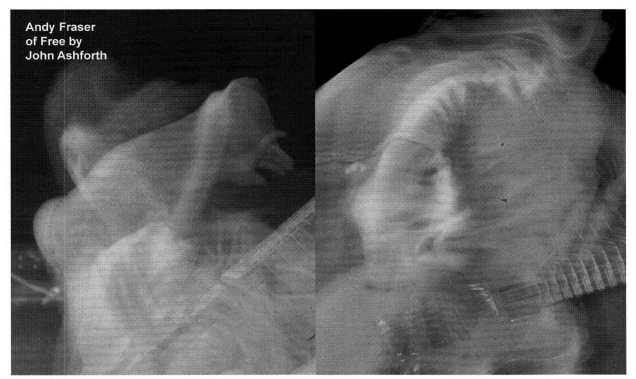

Andy Fraser
of Free by
John Ashforth

experiences; challenging one's perception of reality; questioning fundamental things we take for granted; how we attach meaning to anything.

"I've tasted rarefied air, explored dizzy heights and been under a few tables, although I never acquired the taste nor the stomach for alcohol, and avoided drugs. Somehow being in the world or 'whirled' of art school enticed open the doors of perception without the need to kick them open."

"A few years later, mods in desert boots, grandad vests and parkas, the girls in mini shirts, tank tops and platform shoes, would be snogging at the bus stop..."

If the Grammar School (which he dropped out of) was one of the local centres of the establishment, then he reckons the art school, or Chesterfield College of Art and Design, was quite the opposite:

"Living in Hasland, the art school crowd from Penmore House on Hasland Road, was part of local life. They passed our house every day on their way to the 'Dev' or the 'Mutton'. I witnessed the style transformation over the years from jazz beatniks, to scruffs, to mods and to hippies.

"In the fifties you would see 'intellectuals' or 'philosophers' in tweed suits, brogues and cravats, or arty teddy boys, girls in wide skirts, sketching in the park. In the early sixties you might meet some beatniks in berets and sporting beards, girls in tight skirts and roll neck sweaters, buying *Melody Maker* in the newsagents.

"A few years later, mods in desert boots, grandad vests and parkas, the girls in mini shirts, tank tops

and platform shoes, would be snogging at the bus stop. Then the hippies arrived, in the most colourful tie-dye T-shirts, paisley kaftans and of indeterminate gender.

"I had always been intrigued by these non-conformists, so much that I joined them. The art school was the ideal place for subversion, inner exploration and rebellion to germinate. In my first year I was introduced, sometimes formally, often informally to so wide a range of strands and shades of counter-culture, experimentation and radical thinking that everything on the menu was offered in an on-going taster session.

"Anarchy, atheism, agitprop theatre, eastern mysticism, Marxism, existentialism, logical positivism, Seventh Day Adventism and getting pissed were all entertained. The art school had its share of hedonism; a pursuit associated with the art world for centuries. The sixties simply allowed it to be cranked up a few notches. LSD advocate Dr Timothy Leary had his adherents there too.

Tom Bailey and your author Pete Dodd were no strangers to Penmore House. We took up Saturday 'O' level art classes there because, for some bizarre reason, you couldn't study art and English literature on the same syllabus at school. After several years at an all boys school, it was something of a novelty and a liberation to find ourselves in mixed classes. The names Pauline Ogilvy and Wini Turner spring fondly to mind. What's more, Tom and I both passed our exams. Art school dances and gigs would follow, eventually with us performing at them.

"Western psychedelia swirled around eastern mysticism. Initially it was George Harrison's wife Patti Boyd who, in 1967, introduced George and the rest of the Beatles to the Indian guru, Maharishi Mahesh Yogi and his method of Transcendental Meditation. Through The Beatles, Donovan, Mia Farrow, Mike Love and the Beach Boys the whole world heard about the Maharishi and TM.

"Maharishi told some journalists that John, Paul, George and Ringo were angels, creating a wave of joy and love through the consciousness and hearts of the world."

"Maharishi told some journalists that John, Paul, George and Ringo were angels, creating a wave of joy and love through the consciousness and hearts of the world, melting the post-war misery and coldness with waves of love and ripples of joy. Many of us could feel these waves, some more intensely than others, and wanted to be part of that revolution, helping to push it along.

"The Beatles and one hundred other musicians, artists, writers, film makers all reflected what was happening in the collective consciousness.

"One of my tutors, Steve, a depressive and disillusioned American academic and avant-garde film maker, we noticed, had become less cynical and sarcastic, had stopped drinking and seemed happier. We were impressed. He gave all the credit to Transcendental Meditation and sneakily included an introduction to TM in a series of lectures on 'enhancing creative thinking'.

"Along with about 30 other students, I took instruction in the technique and for the first time in

my life experienced true peace of mind. Perhaps I had been hoping for something like this from Christianity, which describes a state of 'grace'. After two or three days of meditating, this new clarity crystallised while I was riding on the top deck of the 51 bus into town.

"I became aware in a slightly detached way that I was only thinking one thing, clearly and enjoyably, instead of the cacophony of thoughts I was used to. My mind was often like a fuzzy transistor radio with poor reception tuned between several stations. This was like a new hi-fi.

"Some of us are unable to fit in to the moulds organisations and establishments try to push us into. I was fortunate to escape early with only minor psychological bruising. It was more like 'dropping in' to myself than dropping out. 'Finding myself' at art school, in both senses of the expression, was like having a front row view of the transformation of the sixties. Or maybe more like taking part in the show. Even the huge new colour television in the TV room at Penmore House had the colour turned all the way up."

As one of the alternative alumni, John feels fortunate to have taken part in the sixties transformation: "I'm pleased to say that today's generation is having a better time at school. I left school with little more than a confused and empty feeling. Teenage nervous breakdown? No. More of a breakthrough in consciousness and creativity.

"I left art school with two 'A' levels, an English 'O' level, all at top grades, a professional diploma in photography and the equivalent of two BAs, in

Right: Wakefield's Army Stores

graphic design and film making. Later I took an MA in writing studies. Apart from two weeks causing mayhem on the night shift in the Mother's Pride bakery in upper Newbold, I've been able to make my way doing creative work – music, photography, graphic design, film making, scriptwriting, teaching meditation and teaching in art schools and universities.

"Maybe most of all I learned how to live and appreciate so many aspects of life and culture. Spiritual highs and mundane lows – I've enjoyed the endless stillness of ashram life and endured the urgent pressure as a media professional. And it's mostly been fun."

It was at art school that John pursued his love of photography and being a Stop Out kinda guy he combined his passion for the photographic image with his love of live music. He would ask bands at the Vic if he could photograph them and if they said 'yes' he would do.

If he hadn't had a ruthless clear out of old prints and negatives more than a decade ago John would be featured in this book as the only known person to have a photographic record of concerts held in the Victoria Ballroom.

But all is not lost. He made frequent forays to Sheffield for his music fix and captured acts on stage often at the Sheffield University Union building.

John: "The Mucky Duck (Black Swan) in Sheffield was the house of blues, where I saw Vinegar Joe, Chicken Shack, Stone The Crows, Stackridge and more.

"Something was stirring in the collective consciousness of the world. Signs could be seen in all the arts. Also in politics and education..."

"The Sheffield University Students' Union put on an outstanding roster of bands: Free, Deep Purple, Family, Focus, Faces, Terry Reid, Bridget St John, Bob Kerr's Whoopee Band, Roy Harper.

"The Sheffield City Hall was the biggest venue in the area. It's where I saw Black Sabbath, Free, Captain Beefheart and more. I also saw John Martyn, Tom Paxton, Julie Felix, and the Third Ear Band, but I don't remember where. For years I must have attended two or three high quality, live music events every week.

"This was higher education of the highest degree. My tastes broadened and encompassed Indian classical, various styles of jazz, medieval religious and experimental music.

"My violin was replaced by a bass guitar. My step brother, a good-looking young man three years older than me, had been recruited into a local pop group, despite him never having picked up a musical instrument before and not being able to sing.

"He played several gigs, was paid and had blisters to prove it, although the bass was never plugged into an amp. The main point being that a glossy red Egmond bass guitar appeared in our house. After one lesson from a cousin's boyfriend who was a semi-pro bass player, I was away, no stopping me.

"The first band I was in which actually performed was fundamentally a Free tribute band, before tribute bands existed. We played almost everything from their first three albums along with a couple of Stones numbers, one from Argent, Status Quo, Rory Gallagher. We played regularly at the Art School dos."

John observes that during the 1950s a post-war gloom hung over Chesterfield and the whole of northern England. Then the sixties arrived and lifted spirits:

"The sixties was a harbinger of light, like the sun bursting through an overcast sky. My age group probably experienced the transformation more head on, particularly if you were at art school.

"Something was stirring in the collective consciousness of the world. Signs could be seen in all the arts. Also in politics and education – student demonstrations in USA and France; the growth of the civil rights movement; reactions to the assassination of John F. Kennedy in 1963 and Martin Luther King Jnr in 1968; anti Vietnam war demonstrations, were all signs of a major upheaval."

The signs could be seen that change was afoot, even in Chesterfield. Among developments in town, was the new cake-shaped courthouse. Now no longer in use as such, it remains a building listed for its special architectural or historic interest.

The Barbara Hepworth 'tooth' sculpture appeared outside the new AGD offices and at one time in the sixties it developed a Beatle wig in an act of vandalism that either appalled or amused.

The AGD itself – the pensions division of the Post Office – brought hundreds of newcomers to the town, mostly from the south. The Loundsley Green estate on the west side of town was built to accommodate them. John recalls that one of these newcomers, a schoolfriend called Paul, initially thought the locals were all Quakers or religious fundamentalists, because so many people used 'thee' and 'tha' in their everyday language.

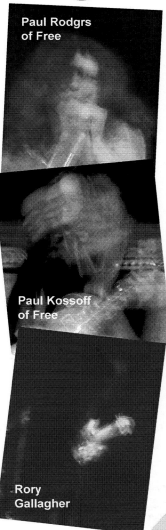

Paul Rodgrs of Free

Paul Kossoff of Free

Rory Gallagher

Above: Photos by John Ashforth

Dirty Old Town

John: "On the bus to town I would enjoy the shapes of Austin Sevens, Vauxhall Crestas, Wolseleys, Humber Hawks, Rileys, Morris and Bedford vans and motor cycle combinations. Passing under Horns Bridge, there was an uneasy feeling that a train might topple on us from one of the lines above.

"Three different tracks overlapped at three levels. Three railway companies had built stations in Chesterfield. The London Midland Railway ran to Scotland or London, the Great Central could take you to Pilsley or even Southport or Cleethorpes and on the Lancashire, Derbyshire & East Coast Railway you could travel to Bolsover and as far as Lincoln.

"In the early sixties, the first person you might meet, as you stepped off the bus at the corner of Vicar Lane, was Bob the war veteran. With a missing limb Bob sold matches from a tray. In his hobnail boots, grey air force greatcoat decorated with medals, his unwashed, battered appearance and gruff voice alarmed people. Children were afraid of him.

"One day we decided to talk to him. He recollected his racehorse veterinary surgeon days before the war and recited the complete bone anatomy of a horse. He left us to dismiss the nearby bus queue, military style in his sergeant major bark, as the uneasy passengers filed on to the bus."

"John Turners was the first department store you would pass on Packers Row. Close by was the Shambles. Wakefield's Army Stores had dazzling window displays, every conceivable space crammed with products; gas masks; sea boot hose; air force officer's silk pyjamas; a tank compass, Swiss Army knives. I bought my first headphones there which had been ripped out of a WW2 bomber."

The Scene

The first teen scene for John was Jimmy's – the parish church youth club on Sunday after evensong choir or altar boy duties had been fulfilled:

"St James Hall was the shabby old Crooked Spire's church hall where, later in 1969, Pink Floyd, Caravan and others would play. It was a huge echoing space and, with a faulty double turntable and PA, about a dozen of us were left to entertain ourselves. Hasland Youth Club was the next step where they held a great disco on Friday nights.

"At school the underground music scene was pulsating – rucksacks were just the right size to hold a few LPs. Tim Searcy, the art master allowed some of us to play records in the art room at lunchtime. Froggy, an old French master complained that orgies were being held.

"John Turners was the first department store you would pass on Packers Row. Close by was the Shambles. Wakefield's Army Stores had dazzling window displays."

"I was so immersed in the music that I was thrown out of the new language lab for recording myself singing *Sunshine Of Your Love* instead of practising French pronunciation. Music was the perfect antidote to the tedium of school.

"The only bands I had seen by then were local lads playing rock and roll and pop at garden parties and youth clubs. One Saturday night my life changed dramatically. It must have been late '68. Mark, a pal from a year or two above told me that the Nice were playing at the Vic on Saturday and he would get me in. You had to be 18. I was 15.

"Their single, *America* was out and I had their album. The radical rearrangements of classical

Right: John Turners

and jazz themes, Bob Dylan songs, and Keith Emerson's showmanship and abuse of the Hammond organ completely blew me away. This was real music — the energy and inventiveness were mind blowing.

"From then on every week I was at the Vic watching a brilliant band: Free, Taste, Yes, Principal Edward's Magic Theatre, Mighty Baby, Van Der Graaf Generator, King Crimson, Mott The Hoople, Jethro Tull, Family, Blossom Toes, Tea & Symphony, Ten Years After, Renaissance, Uriah Heep, Strawbs, Coliseum, Savoy Brown Blues Band, Keef Hartley Band, Junior's Eyes and Elmer Gantry's Velvet Opera, and more.

"Ian, an older friend from Clowne, made a bold step in his role as ents secretary for Chesterfield tech students union by blowing the whole years entertainment budget on staging Pink Floyd at St James Hall in March 1969. Believe it or not there's a bootleg recording of the event on YouTube.

"There was also Chesterfield Folk Club on Friday nights at the Queen's Park Hotel where I watched Martyn Carthy, Bernard Wrigley, Michael Chapman, John Renbourne, Mike Harding, Stefan Grossman, Sandy Denny, Maddy Prior, Roy Harper, Al Stewart and more.

"In 1969 I went to see Fairport Convention at St James Hall with my first girlfriend Tina, but they didn't show up. Days later we heard about their M1 crash. Not far from Scratchwood Services, the van veered off the road and there was a nasty accident with two fatalities, the drummer Martin Lamble, just 19 at the time, and Jeannie Franklyn, Richard Thompson's girlfriend.

"Thompson suffered a broken shoulder and bassist Ashley Hutchings was sent to the hospital with assorted serious injuries, while guitarist Simon Nicol, who'd been sleeping on the floor of the vehicle when it went off the road, escaped with a concussion.

Disco Nights

"I also liked soul and motown and some pop, and the Vic disco nights were the place to go. It was mainly a mod scene. We were mods until the underground scene emerged and we evolved into magic-men or magics.

Ron and Rod of the Faces.

Rod conducts the Sheffield crowd

"Another branch of the mods morphed into skinheads. Chesterfield had its own Brighton, albeit three years later. The tension between the local mods and rockers had been building for weeks and reached straining point one weekend.

"Word had circulated that there was going to be trouble. The bouncers at the Vic had armed themselves with chair legs concealed inside their suit jackets. All the mods were uneasy for about a fortnight until the showdown occurred one Saturday night when the rockers invaded the town centre.

"They swarmed in from surrounding towns and villages, Grassmoor, Pinxton, Duckmanton, Clay Cross, Shirebrook, Eckington, Staveley. A metal-studded, black leathered legion, the width of the High Street swarmed down from Burlington Street towards the Market Square.

"Another branch of the mods morphed into skinheads. Chesterfield had its own Brighton, albeit three years later."

"Seeing them approaching, we didn't stay to watch the event and ran down through the Shambles and Low pavement to the East Midland bus station. We jumped on the first bus leaving town just to get away.

"The mini-men from Nottingham often visited the Red Lion Disco on Vicar Lane on Sunday evenings. You knew they were in town from the line of ten, 12 or 14 red minis parked in a row along Vicar Lane, often modded with lowered roofs, wide wheels and spats."

A Room For Romance

If you were of a certain age in the sixties, romance was an urgent item on the agenda.

John: "Tina and I met at the Vic Taste gig. I had been in the Commercial (on the junction of Vicar Lane and South Street, one of the pubs where a 15-year-old could drink without being thrown out, although an older looking friend would go to the bar) with a bunch of pals before the gig and had a half of beer which had emboldened me enough to allow Tina and me to get off with each other.

"Teen romance blossomed with Tina, who was a year older, at Tapton School and had a mischievous sense of humour. We would hang out at the YMCA coffee bar on Holywell Street or at a friend's where we babysat sometimes. It was early summer and Tina was at home revising for 'O' levels. She invited me round one day when her parents were at work.

"That afternoon Tina helped me make great strides in overcoming my shyness. Her books remained on the bedroom floor. We were dozing blissfully with Leonard Cohen singing on the record player, Hey, *That's No Way to Say*

Goodbye, when she jolted off the bed and ran to the window. Tina's dad had arrived home early from work and was walking up the long, front garden path.

"If it had been winter, with more clothes to put on, I wouldn't have made it. I leapt down the stairs, stood at the front door and as he came in through the back door, Tina signalled to me and I shot down the garden path, leapt over the front wall and walked home in a mood of beguiling and nervous contentment, as though I'd just appeared in a scene from *The Graduate*.

"The first gift I gave Tina was the *Rock Machine – I Love You* album. It was a sampler released by CBS and had such a rich and varied collection of music that it climbed to 15 in the LP charts. Most of all it gave a taste of the wonderful range of new American music emerging. And it only cost ten bob which I could just about afford from my Saturday job at Jacksons bakery in Hasland.

"I think I had given Tina the record as a Valentine's present. It's equally successful precursor, *The Rock Machine Turns You On*, would have been just as appropriate."

Back At Art School

After hearing a lecture by a Marxist general studies lecturer, within weeks you could find John selling Socialist Worker newspaper in Chesterfield Market Place:

"I was hauled up before the principal, Arthur Pears (whose only accolade was designing a jelly mould for the royals) for holding political meetings on college premises without permission and without inviting representatives from the opposing side.

"I asked for permission and invited him to represent the other side but he declined. My brief flirtation with the extreme left was soon cut short when it became apparent that many of their leaders and organisers were prepared for a violent overthrow. Fear, anger, aggression and destruction seemed to be a fundamental motivation in them. This was not for me. It was all a far cry from the ideals of the sixties: equality; freedom of speech; true democracy; an end to war. You cannot fight for a peaceful world.

"A number of staff and students fully embraced the new hedonism of the sixties, with a decadent indulgences of Roman proportions. Jeff, my history of art lecturer, had wholeheartedly subscribed to the more traditional artist's way of life – getting pissed. Jeff had enjoyed a temporary, between the wars period of fame as a painter, yet he'd lost an arm in a childhood accident. 'But for drinking and painting you only need one,' he said. Only at art school could you be in a cricket team with a one-armed, alcoholic batsman who was, oddly enough, also a good bowler."

Knight In White Plimsolls

Richard Knight would also eventually follow the art school route, studying in Leeds where his fellow students included Green Gartside from Scritti Politti (with whom he appeared on Top of the Pops), and Marc Almond of Soft Cell. Several years before that he was busy establishing his own personal foundation course.

Richard: "In 1967 I so wanted to be part of the Summer of Love. I'd read about it in the News of The World at my grandmas. Donovan and Paul McCartney talking about LSD – meditation and 'be-ins'.

"I bought Arnold Layne and played the flip side, *Candy and a Currant Bun* – lysergic messages scrambled inside pop songs. I badly wanted in. I was 12 years old and ready to smoke banana skins. I ate sugar cubes and imagined.

"Me and my friends hung out on a wall beside the Mobil garage on Brockwell Lane. It was the place to be. Feeling the moment, I declared we should become Flower Children.

"I took my pals off to the waste ground behind the garage to get flowers and create our look. No one else was really that interested. I picked a wild rose and stuck it behind my ear. I could feel something crawling. A friend started to laugh. An earwig exited the flower. I pulled at the rose and the earwig fell out too. My first lesson in the dark side of the

hippie dream. Unperturbed, I bought beads from a stall on the market, a floral shirt...

"I hung out at the bowling alley playing Prince Buster on the jukebox – 'Al Capone's guns don't argue'. Hipsters: brown checks and scratchy, big buckle belt, skinny rib acrylic jumper. Out went the John Lennon cap and the Johnny Kidd striped top... I felt I had joined the demi-monde."

By 1968 Richard had joined the throng in town that paraded the High Street, gathering at Bobby Cousin's corner:

"At 13, we weren't 'faces' and didn't quite make the scene. I'd bought Levis from the Co-op and a denim jacket and desert boots.

"We would walk down to the Market Hall, hang around Hudsons, gaze at exotic packs of cigarettes in the glass faced kiosk, buy ten Number Six between us and walk back.

"Meanwhile, it was Friday night, upstairs at the The Eagle on Newbold Moor, just old enough to attend a youth club. I watched mod girls dancing in formation to *This Is Soul*. Moves executed in a disinterested, cool style. A line of mini skirts, small moves, faces composed in studied boredom.

"While mods were the initial reference point in 1966-68, all tiger tail Lambretta 200s and fish tail parkas, by 1968-69 we were busy growing our hair, or attempting to. 'We' being me, at 13 or 14, and a handful of rebels and miscreants at school. The

Richard 'Ricky' Knight and Tom Bailey a few years later at the final Windsor Free Festival which earned notoriety when it was broken up at dawn on the sixth day by hundreds of truncheon wielding officers from the Thames Valley police. The level of force used led several national newspapers to call for an inquiry, and Roy Jenkins, the Home Secretary, to request a report from the Thames Valley Chief Constable.

majority were happy to conform. (The regulation haircut at school was one inch above the shirt collar. We were lined up outside the gym, our hair measured with a ruler.)

"I found a place with the alienated and disengaged. We skived gym and long distance running, stuck paperbacks in our blazer pockets and carried vinyl to and from school. Unlike some of our compatriots, we didn't transform into Skins, we adopted greatcoats, an old trilby, white plimsolls a la John Lennon, Levis, dyed granddad vests from Wakefield's. We smoked herbal tobacco, drank cider and sherry in the corner of a field, sat trance-like in darkened corners nodding meaningfully to Atomic Rooster, Led Zeppelin 1 and 2, Taste *On The Boards*, Van Der Graff Generator *H to He*, Graham Bond's *Holy Magick* and Third Ear Band's *Alchemy,* Humble Pie or Bonzo Dog, The Who, John and Yoko or Wild Man Fischer.

"At Sheffield City Hall in 1969 between the release of *Music From A Doll's House* and *Family Entertainment* Roger Chapman, like a shaman, stands transcendent. In my great coat and plimmies, I nod appropriately to Family's *The Weaver's Answer*.

"My first pair of jeans I got were from Yeomans. The smell of that shop is still in my memory, a combination of starch, canvas and rubber."

A flashback to 1962: "A fair came to a spinney near where I lived (behind The Moonrakers pub on Keswick Drive). I was just turned seven and newly able to play out on my own. I hung out at the fair every night even before it opened.

"Fragments of memory remain: girls in Capri pants being teased by boys with pompadours about their beehives. Beehives piled improbably high. Girls screaming with laughter, the rumble of the Waltzer, the electric blue hum of the dodgems and Del Shannon, Bobby Vee, Bobby Darin, Bill Haley kickin' out behind.

"The night air full of burning diesel and hot oil, I took a deep breath. Some girls came up and started on me. One had knelt behind me and the one in my face pushed me over. They took the leather wallet with my spendo in. I dusted myself off. A few minutes later one of them came back, checked I was OK and gave me back my wallet. Quite an evening.

"My first pair of jeans I got were from Yeomans. The smell of that shop is still in my memory, a combination of starch, canvas and rubber. Tek-Sac jeans and Tek-Sac jacket. I was a made man.

Seven years old and, in my fantasy, somewhere between Mike Mercury and Little Joe – Supercar and Bonanza; my world.

On to 1964 and it's time for Richard to buy his first album – at just eight years old: "I broke my arm at school and as a sort of compensation I was given money by relatives. I spent 32/6d on The Rolling Stones in Mono on Decca Records and played it every day over and over on a blue and cream Dansette.

"Record covers function like a bulletin board of what's happening. I devoured Rave magazine, Jackie, NME, whatever was available. I didn't see the Avengers, I didn't get to see The Beatles at the City Hall but I studied the Rolling Stones EP Five By Five cover like it was the Dead Sea Scrolls and had to have a Breton top like the one Mick has on the back. I did the quiz in Rave. Was I a mod or a rocker? Maybe I was a 'mocker', like says Ringo in *A Hard Days Night*?

"My auntie liked the new 'beat music' and took me to Sheff City Hall to see various packages: The Nashville Teens, The Kinks, Rockin' Berries, Dave Berry, Dave Clark Five, Manfred Man, Bill Halley and the Comets, hundreds of girls screaming, throwing sweets. Seeing the Dave Clark Five do showbiz/cabaret numbers killed it. That wasn't what I wanted.

"The Kinks, in contrast, were wild and beautiful. Their hair was truly 'long' for the time and their mock Tudor jackets, tight trousers and Cuban heels looked funky. Girls threw Opal Fruits at The Kinks (Jelly Babies at The Beatles) Sharp corners must have hurt."

Wizard, by Richard Knight

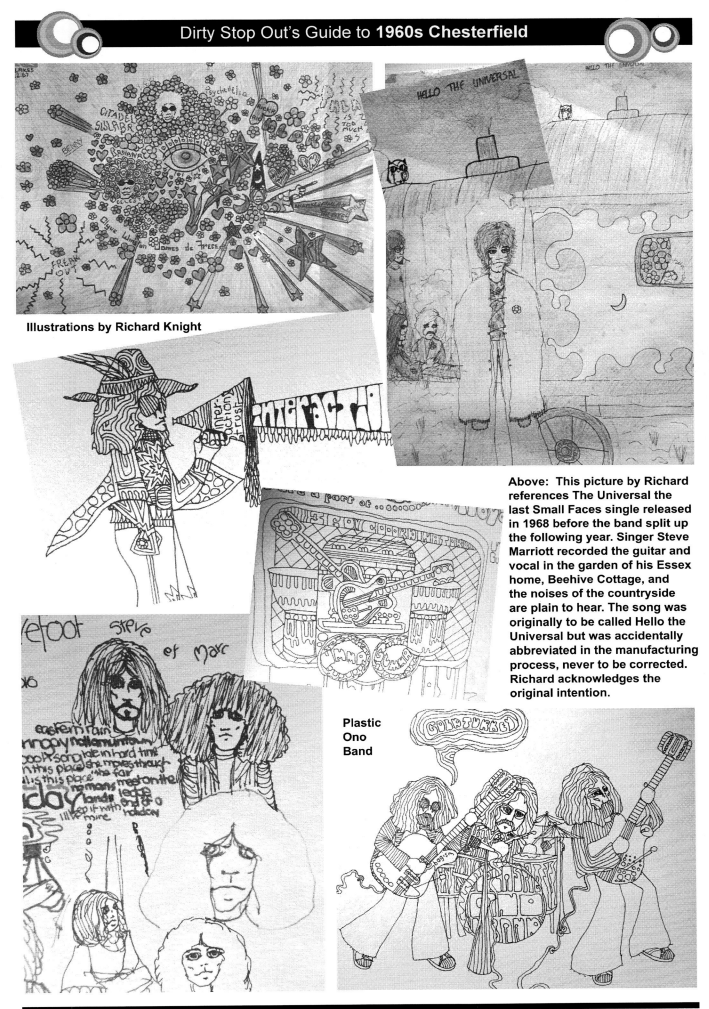

Illustrations by Richard Knight

Above: This picture by Richard references The Universal the last Small Faces single released in 1968 before the band split up the following year. Singer Steve Marriott recorded the guitar and vocal in the garden of his Essex home, Beehive Cottage, and the noises of the countryside are plain to hear. The song was originally to be called Hello the Universal but was accidentally abbreviated in the manufacturing process, never to be corrected. Richard acknowledges the original intention.

Plastic Ono Band

CHAPTER 13

MY FIRST LONG PLAYING RECORD

Right: Fab 208 magazine August 13, 1966. Brimming with full colour pics of all the stars. and Disc and Music Echo from February 1967. Dusty Springfield and Petula Clark feature on the front.

Your author Pete Dodd relives the agony and excitement of buying his first LP: "I grew up on Shaftesbury Avenue in Ashgate. I remember walking up the road, along Springfield Avenue and Welfare Avenue to pick up a copy of the music magazine Fab 208 from the newsagent at the end of Barker Lane on Chatsworth Road. I was 12.

"It featured full colour 'posters' of the stars and in the mid to late sixties employed celebrity guest editors such as Donovan, Cat Stevens, Gerry Marsden, The Kinks and Dave Dee, Dozy, Beaky, Mick and Tich to boost the magazine's profile. It was the first of its type to cover other popular culture topics like fashion, films and television, as well as music.

"I gaped at the stars of the day – Sandie Shaw,

"I gaped at the stars of the day – Sandie Shaw, Lulu and Tom Jones in all their showbiz glamour – and then at the much more 'real' Small Faces with their small, genuinely spotty young faces."

Lulu and Tom Jones in all their showbiz glamour – and then at the much more 'real' Small Faces with their small, genuinely spotty young faces. How could a pimply young lad not fall in love with everything they represented?

"I probably bought the magazine because its title referenced the broadcast frequency of the Great 208 Radio Luxembourg commercial station. Based, as the name suggests, on mainland Europe it was the only way to bypass the Beeb and was a precursor to the pirate stations (eg Caroline and London) that would begin broadcasting from ships anchored off the UK coast later in the decade.

"Often-as-not via a transistor radio earpiece under the blankets after bedtime, Luxembourg would

deliver the hits of the day and interesting non-chart bound sounds through programmes such as *Battle of the Bands*. It was here I was introduced to the first two singles by Pink Floyd – *Arnold Layne* (about a clothes line underwear thief) and *See Emily Play*, both the work of gifted psychedelic songwriter and Floyd front man Syd Barrett. And the band, though a standard guitar, organ, bass and drums combo, seemed to sound magically otherwise and more so than the sum of its parts.

"By now I was aged 13 and had progressed from *Fab 208* to *Disc and Music Echo*. Studying the charts I would learn that in addition to the ubiquitous Sgt Pepper from the omnipresent Beatles and The Sound of Music soundtrack there were other musical wonders clamouring for my attention. The one that stood out for me was Floyd's debut, the charmingly titled *The Piper at the Gates of Dawn* (after a chapter in Kenneth Grahame's *Wind in the Willows*).

"It should be noted at this point that the 'album' as it was commonly known (and still is), was so called because it referred to a collection of already existing songs gathered together, like snap shots of past moments, for perusal in one place. As such, many of them were a minority attraction for committed fans of the artist in question.

"But the emerging acts of the sixties were beginning to elevate the long playing format to the status of high art as they used the medium to create ambitious new works paying little heed to the comings and goings of the hit parade.

"So it was that, after some hard pocket money saving, an excited young lad set off to Hudsons clutching his 32/6d, soon parting with it for a 12-inch square parcel of potential wonderment to be savoured after dashing home.

"Neither single was on the album so the music was completely unknown. Placing the record on the green felt turntable mat and lowering the stylus arm to the vinyl created a moment of intense anticipation. You will learn in due course that a record of depth and imagination reveals itself over time and repeated listens. But that wisdom was not available to an excited and impatient 13-year-old.

"Twenty minutes later, as the stylus tracked off to the central groove of side one, I was left perplexed and confused by six initially impenetrable tracks. Flipping the disc, side two started with *Interstellar Overdrive* – a nine-minute avant garde instrumental opus bearing no relation to anything I

"I was lost. The bitter tears of immense disappointed stung my cheeks as I struggled to make sense of the unsettling world I had entered. And to make matters worse I seemed to have forked out a small fortune – more or less my complete wealth in the world – on a complete dud."

had ever heard before in my life or could possibly imagine would even exist.

"I was lost. The bitter tears of immense disappointed stung my cheeks as I struggled to make sense of the unsettling world I had entered. And to make matters worse I seemed to have forked out a small fortune – more or less my complete wealth in the world – on a complete dud.

"It's at times like this that it is fortunate if you have a kind and understanding father nearby. I was that lucky lad and would be until I reached 19 when he died after a stroke.

"Dad had a listen to the mind-boggling *Interstellar Overdrive* and concluded (probably having simply read and understood the title) that the intro riff represented a space ship taking off and the return of the riff at the end suggested said ship touching down at journey's end and what came in between was a cosmic journey through time and space. Thanks dad. You turned the tide.

"Furthermore, what followed Overdrive was a series of highly approachable almost child like tunes including *The Gnome, Scarecrow* and *Bike*. Jackpot.

"Suffice to say, further listens revealed layer after layer of undiluted pleasure and what had first seemed unapproachable became a high benchmark by which to judge everything else. No

longer a dud, but quite possibly the best record ever made!

Sometime later dad bought me a Dave Brubeck EP – I guess he thought I'd grown up enough to understand. The highlight was the impeccable *Take Five* in which a beautiful tune is laid over the 'awkward' time signature of 5/4. But so you'd hardly notice. Masterful. The disc also featured *Blue Rondo a la Turk* in 9/8 time (nicked uncredited by Keith Emserson for the Nice in 1967 who converted it to standard 4/4 time) and a version of *Deep in the Heart of Texas* where the drums on the intro hint at the melody to come. Far out. My adventures in music were underway."

Pink Floyd in 1967 the year Piper was released.

Left: Syd Barrett in sharp focus with the rest of the band a blur. In reality it was the other way round.

Left: Pink Floyd's debut album The Piper at the Gates of Dawn released August 4, 1967.

CHAPTER 14

PERFORMANCE

If it wasn't for the players of the day, there would have been nothing for the punters to enjoy. One player who has been keeping Chesterfield and beyond entertained for most of his life is drummer Stuart 'Nip' Heeley.

As far as David McPhie was concerned Nip was one of the most accomplished drummers in town back in the sixties. David: "He went on to have a great career. He would, of all the local musicians I came across, have fitted seamlessly into the line-up of most of the successful British rock bands of the era."

Even at 16 years old Nip was desperate to get performing. And his 'big break' came when the drummer's stool in the Envoys became vacant. Soon after the name was changed to Harry Griebson's String Band.

Nip: "The Envoys were playing covers of chart stuff at the time, Four Tops, Wilson Pickett, etc., and played lots of working men's clubs, miners' welfares and pubs. I remember lots of Sheffield

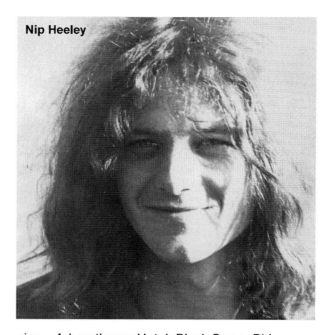

Nip Heeley

gigs – Arbourthorne Hotel; Black Swan; Birley Hotel; Cannon Hall, Firvale, etc. Singer Bob Skelland had a great voice, and bassist Mick Cook had a habit of dancing on tables whilst playing, unwise in places such as Carr Vale or Staveley!

"If my memory serves me correctly, the original suggestion from Mick for the band's name was Harry Griebson's Rag Time Jam Orchestra, which became shortened (thankfully) to Harry Griebson's String Band, then to Harry Griebson, which in turn became plain Griebson. If we hadn't broken up when we did it would no doubt have become Grie!"

Replacing a member of an already gigging band saw Nip off to a flying start: "I got on a train that was already going. After the first gig they were dropping me off at home and they said: 'Here's your money'. And I remember saying: 'Oh no I don't want any money'. I was doing what I'd always dreamed of doing and that was enough."

When not gigging and rehearsing, Nip used to hang around Hudson's 'singles bar' in the Market Hall with friends soaking up all the new sounds and occasionally raiding his paper round tin to splash out on a disc: "Mrs Hudson used to shoo us away because we would be just hanging around there.

"But when the Some Kinda Mushroom shop opened you were actually encouraged to hang around. You'd go in and sit and have a cup of tea and talk about music. It was a brilliant place."

And it was shop owner David McPhie who

Nip playing his Olympic kit, age 15, in his bedroom at his parents' house in Wingerworth. Nip: "Note the orthodox grip, I soon changed to the matched grip when I had to compete with Bob's and John Hallam's AC30s after joining The Envoys."

became Harry Griebson's manager noting that it was difficult for Northern bands writing and performing their own material to secure enough gigs to survive on the circuit.

A failed attempt to secure a recording contract with Island Records proved a memorable experience. Nip: "We were invited to record a demo at Island's recording studio in a lovely Victorian villa in Hammersmith's St Peter's Square. The coolest record company in the country!

"Picking up Bob from his home in Grassmoor on the big day he emerged carrying a basket full of his dad's homing pigeons to release at Newport Pagnell services!

"Sparks were big at the time and were rehearsing in the studio next to us, and we saw Ronnie Lane (of Faces and Small Faces fame) in the local pub."

Sadly for Nip, Island narrowed down their choice of signings to the Griebson's or 'blue-eyed soul singer' Jess Roden, and Roden won out.

Nip achieved iconic status in town when he got the drummer's job with hit maker Gilbert O'Sullivan touring the UK and Eire and has played with a host of artists over the decades including: Dave Berry and the Cruisers, The Albion Band, Ashley Hutchings, an early incarnation of Saxon called SOB (Son of a Bitch), The Actors, with singer/guitarist Paul Hopkinson, and Lisahall (named after the band's Danesmoor singer, Lisa Hall, also with Paul Hopkinson).

Nip: "We were signed by Reprise Records in Los Angeles, and the title track of our record *Is This Real?* is featured in the Nicole Kidman/Sandra Bullock film *Practical Magic.*"

Nip has spent time living in London – in Pimlico not far from where the Small Faces had earlier lived in 'moddish' splendour, and in France. This century he is recognised by many as half of the powerhouse rhythm section – along with Mick

An early gig.

Twelves on bass – with the hugely popular covers band The Pitz, featuring Paul Hopkinson and Rob Lee on guitars and vocals. They went their separate ways in 2017. Since then Paul and Rob have regrouped as the anagram ziPt, gigging extensively in the area.

Right: This is an original hand-drawn (probably by Roger Buck) and faded poster from the Vic when Harry Griebson's supported Family. Note that at this stage the Velvet Underground had become the Harlem Highway. Nip added the '1968' date reference much later to remind him of when it was.

The Envoys pictured in Grassmoor in 1968. Vocalist/guitarist Bob Skelland also played bass guitar for Shape of the Rain at a later date. Nip: "John Hallam, in striped shirt playing a Fender Stratocaster, subsequently left and we concentrated on original music and became Harry Griebson's String Band.

This shot of Harry Griebsons String Band at Weston Park in Sheffield was published on the front page of the Sheffield Morning Telegraph the following day sometime in 1969.

MENTIONED IN DISPATCHES

Fondly remembered Chesterfield musician Jon Stoppard was a familiar face on the scene. In the early 1970s one of his many musical projects earned him a certain cult status. Under the name The Equinox, Stoppard on keyboards, along with (the legendary) Mick Shedd on vocals and guitar, Sid Oldfield on bass

and Terry Waldon on drums recorded an album called Hard Rock.

As the title suggests it is a reflection of the developing sounds of the day echoing the likes of Deep Purple, Black Sabbath and Led Zeppelin and is described by Forced Exposure Mail Order thus: "Although it must be said that our youngsters can't match the playing skills of the bands they mirrored, it's justice to state Hard Rock is a more than decent effort, and a true rarity even for the connoisseurs of the genre."

Released on the budget Boulevard label, to add to the cultish mystery, the front cover featured 'a band' that bore no relation to the players involved – a stock shot of four 'happening' people.

A versatile player, Stoppard could just as easily turn his hand to, say, the lyrical compositions of the blind Irish harpist Turlough O'Carolan. For the curious, many examples of his work can be found on Soundcloud.

The three schoolfriends, who would go on to form the Thompson Twins, all first picked up guitars as young teenagers in the mid-sixties learning the songs and licks of the day and jamming the blues with friends. It was a decade later that Tom Bailey, John Roog and (your author) Pete Dodd regrouped and formed the band with the addition of young drummer Jon Podgorski. Gigs followed in town at the AGD, the Highfields, the Rugby Club and various other rooms above pubs and restaurants. Sheffield had a vibrant live music scene in the post-punk seventies and the TTs became regulars at the Broadfield pub, the Uni and the Limit Club, where the band attracted it's first (and favourable) national review thanks to the NME. Minus Jon, the other three

decided to chuck in the day jobs and head off to the big city. Here are some Chesterfield shots showing the band (rather blurred) in a one-off gig at the Civic Theatre, now the Pomegranate. The cardboard cut-out guest guitarist is Nick Lowe, with battery powered strumming arm, a promotional device borrowed from Stu Smith's SKM just around the corner.

Right: Rehearsals at the attic at the band's Cromwell Rd HQ.

Left: "Ooooh Thompson." That was the line they sang – the legendary Thompsonettes, T Crowley and Helen Richardson.

ACKNOWLEDGEMENTS

A big thank you to all the contributors named in the text who made this book possible, your input has been invaluable. And to Rob Busby for eagle-eyed proof reading in the early stages.

Special thanks must go to David McPhie who worked on this project before me and was kind enough to give access to his manuscript. In fact I'd written for this book before I became its official author! David did not simply abandon the project,

he decided to concentrate on a much more detailed and exhaustive account of the era, its musicians and its venues: *Sounds in the Shadow of the Crooked Spire*. Although the two books occupy similar ground – especially where David's own exploits are concerned – where possible I have used different voices to tell the story of life in Chesterfield during the 1960s. But some of his initial work for this *Stop Out's Guide* inevitably remains.

THE AUTHOR

The Dirty Stop Out's Guide to 1960s Chesterfield **is written by Pete Dodd – former Derbyshire Times journalist and founder member of the Thompson Twins. After his years in the Thompson Twins he remained in London and returned to writing mostly as an entertainment journalist. He moved back to Chesterfield in the Noughties where he continued as a freelance entertainment writer and co-authored two books on music –** *100 Best-Selling Albums of the 80s* **and** *100 Best-Selling Albums of the 90s.* **He is now 'semi-retired' and celebrating the completion of this book. But he never lost sight of music – even if he only briefly made a living out of it. Here are a few images of his exploits over the decades:**

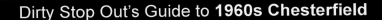

1. Bold Rodney in the early seventies at the Bold Rodney pub on Chatsworth Road from whence they took their name – now the Dynasty Chinese restaurant. From l-r: brothers Pat and Paul Gambles, Pete Dodd, Paul Hague, Chris Drew and Mark Jinkinson.

2. Early 80s with the Thompson Twins headlining at the Lyceum in London (l-r): Pete Dodd, Joe Leeway, and John Roog. And backstage afterwards with Roog and Dodd. Pics: Colin M Howe.

3. Post-Thompson trio Big View with Roog, Crowley and Dodd. One single, August Grass, reached No.8 in the City Limits chart – no big deal as City Limits was a London listings mag in the 1980s.

4. Entertainment journalism in the 1990s: With Reeves and Mortimer at a BBC 'jolly'. And a leisurely Soho lunch with fellow journo Tom Ferguson (right) and Buzzcocks stalwarts Steve Diggle and Pete Shelley. They were promoting a new album.

5. Full circle. I am now in The Flow an instrumental acoustic trio with my old musical playmates Paul Hague (Bold Rodney) and John Roog (TTs).
A couple of years back we returned to Stainsby and entered the singers' competition. We came a respectable second – no mean feat as none of us sing!

C. E. HUDSON & SON LT.D

NEW RECORD &
HI-FI DEPARTMENTS
OPENING SHORTLY

The original Hudsons
(right) in the process
of moving to its new
store on the left

The legendary Hudsons – supplier of vinyl, instruments, sheet music and more in 1960s Chesterfield.